PERSUADING
ARISTOTLE

PERSUADING ARISTOTLE

The timeless art of persuasion in business, negotiation and the media

PETER THOMPSON

ALLEN & UNWIN

First published in 1998 by
Allen & Unwin
9 Atchison Street
St Leonards NSW 1590
Australia
Phone: (61 2) 8425 0100
Fax: (61 2) 9906 2218
E-mail: frontdesk@allen-unwin.com.au
Web: http://www.allen-unwin.com.au

National Library of Australia
Cataloguing-in-Publication entry:

Thompson, Peter, 1952–
Persuading Aristotle.

Bibliography.
Includes index.

ISBN 186448 739.9.

1. Persuasion (Psychology). 2. Persuasion (Rhetoric).
3. Interpersonal communication. I. Title.

153.852

Set in 12/16 pt Weiss by DOCUPRO, Sydney
Printed and bound by Griffin Press Pty Ltd, Adelaide

10 9 8 7 6 5 4 3 2 1

CONTENTS

1   How persuasion works: What Aristotle taught   1

2   Thinking and organising   14

3   Persuasive language   38

4   How to persuade different personalities   60

5   Step-by-step business presentations   87

6   The astute negotiator   131

7   Dealing with the media   166

Further reading   212

Index   213

For Lissa — My love

CHAPTER 1

HOW PERSUASION WORKS: WHAT ARISTOTLE TAUGHT

1 Background
2 What Aristotle taught

3 'Artistic' persuasion
4 John Bell

> *The fool tells me his reasons. The wise man persuades me with my own.*
>
> Aristotle

> Contra negantem principia non est disputandum.
> *You cannot argue with someone who denies the first principles.*
>
> Anon.

EVERYTHING WE KNOW about the art of persuasion today in our mass marketing era is a legacy of thinkers who lived 2400 years ago. They knew it all! The way we think and persuade today owes everything to the insights of Aristotle and his contemporaries. We are under the influence of Aristotle each time we turn on the television. Advertisers organise the text of their 30-second commercials on the basis of the structures taught at Aristotle's Lyceum. Directors and film writers structure their plots in the same way. Film actors spend years learning the same art of 'delivery' that Aristotle taught as a central element of persuasion.

In television news, politicians and other leaders seek to

1

influence public opinion. Those who understand the power of what Aristotle called 'style' and metaphor do best. Television and radio interviews are conducted in the basic interactive framework adopted by both Socrates and modern interviewers to discover the truth.

In business, the corporate doctors known as management consultants borrow directly from Aristotle's teaching about the 'invention', which is the process of getting to the core question in the diagnosis of the ills of the company they are studying. They report to their clients using Aristotle's 'arrangement' for structuring their arguments.

At school and university, teachers and professors transfer the fundamental learning strategies of Greek logic and thought. Perhaps they teach in the Socratic style. In the social sciences, the dialectical system of Aristotle is the basis for testing the different interpretations of reality. Our courts model themselves on Greek dialectical methods as evidence is presented to prove a case. The evidence is tested by Socratic cross-examination.

So, in many different areas of contemporary life, we are still putting on Aristotle's thinking cap.

Background

Aristotle, Socrates and Plato were the three greatest minds in ancient Greece. Socrates (c. 469–399BC) left no writings but we know about him through the dialogues of Plato. His legacy is the Socratic method of reaching an answer through a dialogue of questioning or cross-examination, and arriving at the truth by discerning the differences between opposite points of view. It is, for example, the prosecution and defence method of our justice and court system, and the foundation of the method of learning pioneered at the Harvard Law and Business Schools and taught widely in Australian universities.

Plato (c. 429–347BC) was Socrates' great disciple. In the *Phaedo*, he described Socrates as 'the wisest and justest and best of all men I have ever known'. At some time in the 380s, Plato set up a school of learning and philosophy, known as the Academy. His most renowned student was Aristotle, who joined him at the age of seventeen and remained until Plato's death. Then Aristotle left Athens to become tutor to a 13-year-old Macedonian prince, later known as Alexander the Great.

Aristotle returned to Athens in 338BC and founded his own school in the gymnasium of the Lyceum in 335BC. There, for twelve years, he taught under a covered walk, known as a *peripatos*, his students becoming known as peripatetics. In the afternoons, he would teach rhetoric—which he called the art of persuasion, 'an ability in each case to see the available means of persuasion'. The Greek word *rhetor* meant public speaker and the origins of the word *rhetorike* date back to Socrates' era.

Plato was greatly disturbed by techniques which had the effect of making the weaker argument the stronger. He was convinced these means were used to build an unjust case against Socrates.

He rejected the injustice which flows from verbal trickery, blaming deceptions on the 'wise men' known as sophists, the most famous of whom, Protagoras, believed that there were no universal truths. 'Man is the measure of all things' was the belief of Protagoras, 'of things that are in so far as they are and of things that are not in so far as they are not'. If nothing is known for sure, therefore, the art of rhetoric becomes decisive in swaying the populace to arrive at conclusions and make judgments. Sophists specialised in teaching the methods of argument.

Socrates was plunged into this dubious moral context to defend his life at a trial which took place in a politically unstable interval following the conclusion of war with Sparta. Accused of blasphemy and corrupting the morals of youth through heretical teachings, Socrates became something of a scapegoat for the declining power of Athens. At his trial, arguments honed by the sophists prevailed and Socrates was condemned to death. He declined an opportunity to escape and committed suicide by drinking hemlock. In the *Apology*, Plato confronts the evil use of oratory as he records Socrates' address to the judges who have condemned him:

> Perhaps you think, O Athenians, that I have been convicted through the want of arguments, by which I might have persuaded you, had I thought it right to do and say anything so that I might escape punishment. Far otherwise: I have been convicted through want indeed, yet not of arguments, but of audacity and impudence, and of the inclination to say such things to you as would have been most agreeable for you to hear, had I lamented and bewailed and done and said many other things unworthy of me, as I affirm, but such as you are accustomed to hear from others . . . But I should much rather choose to die having so defended myself than to live in that way.
>
> (*Translation from Lewis Copeland and Lawrence W. Lamm (eds),*
> The World's Greatest Speeches,
> *New York: Dover Publications, 1973.*)

The miscarriage of justice at the trial of Socrates carried profound lessons about the use of language and emotion for purposes of evil, as well as good.

What Aristotle Taught

In Athens, learning the art of persuasion had great practical purpose. The institutions of the city functioned on rhetoric and persuasion. In the Greek courts, unlike those of Rome, the accused had to defend themselves. Robust debate was also a feature of the people's assembly, or *ecclesia*, which was open to all free-born Athenian men. It was in this context that Aristotle composed *The Art of Rhetoric*, or *On Rhetoric* which appeared around 335BC. Classical rhetoric was divided into five principles or parts. Four of those principles, the elements identified by Aristotle in *On Rhetoric*, remain the foundations of modern persuasion. Another principle, which required memorisation of the text, is no longer fashionable.

The Five Principles

1 *Invention*

'Invention' is about identifying the central question which lies at the heart of the issue being addressed and marshalling the most persuasive arguments to answer it. The answer comes in the form of direct evidence such as witnesses and contracts, and through 'artistic' devices by which the speaker builds an argument based on *ethos* or character, *logos* or reasoning, and *pathos* or passion.

2 *Arrangement*

'Arrangement' is about how to structure and order an argument. What is the strongest point? What should come first, second, third and so on in the way a case is made? 'Arrangement' is the thinking and organising framework for presenting a case. It is the key to the coherence and the flow of an argument. Knowing which framework to apply is the most valuable shortcut in the preparation of any formal communication.

3 Style

'Style' involves choosing the most persuasive and evocative language to make your case. It is not just what you have to say which is important but what words you use to express your thoughts. Style is making choices about words (diction) and putting the words into sentences (composition). Grand, middle and plain styles were identified. Aristotle called meta-phor—that is, expressing something in terms of something else—'the most important thing by far'. Nevertheless, 'it will still be lacking in impact unless it is seasoned with the salt of wit'. Today we know that tapping into the imaginative power of the right side of our brain is the best way to create style through the use of metaphor.

4 Memory

'Memory' refers to the Greek–Roman habit of memorising speeches. I don't recommend memorising text beyond a few key sentences such as your opening and closing lines. When you memorise, you get too fixated with recalling what you have to say rather than putting the focus on getting your message across.

5 Delivery

'Delivery' is about aligning your voice and body language with your message. It is not just what you say and how you express yourself that count, but also how you express yourself non-verbally. Aristotle divided delivery into control of voice and gestures.

Non-verbal communication reveals your real emotional state. It is hard to trick an audience. If your words say one thing and your body and voice are saying something else, no one will be convinced by your words. People believe what your body and voice are saying. The great actor Jimmy Stewart recalled how, in his first feature film, *The Murder Man*, in 1935, 'I was all hands and feet, and didn't know what to do with either'. Actors train to make their act fluent. So should speakers.

Without doubt, we share one thing in common with those who lived in Aristotle's day. Speaking under performance pressure gives people the collywobbles! Speaking in the Athenian *ecclesia* must have been the same nerve-wracking experience that speaking in a presentation, to the media or in a negotiation is today. The good news is that there are techniques to help address these anxieties. They will be discussed in Chapter 5, on business presentations.

Aristotle's principles, with the exception of memory, remain the core issues in persuasive communication today. They make up much of the subject matter of this book and have equal bearing on how we make business presentations, communicate in the media and negotiate.

Artistic Persuasion

Aristotle said that you can persuade someone through direct evidence such as producing witnesses and documents, or through the use of *ethos*, *logos* and *pathos*—the so-called 'artistic' persuasion. An audience can be persuaded by a speaker's character (*ethos*), by the reasoning of their argument (*logos*) and by the speaker's passion (*pathos*). Like a triangle, they form a unity (see Figure 1.1). You can't succeed by applying one and not the other two principles

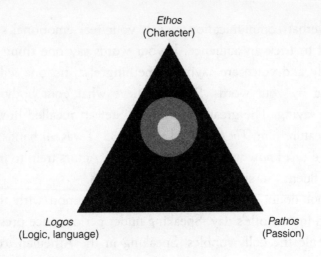

Figure 1.1 Aristotle's Rhetoric

Being persuasive is really about speaking from your heart, your head and your soul.

Ethos or Character

Greek thinking about persuasion began with ethos, meaning character, but what is character? My father used to call it reputation. Your reputation, he said, means everything in your business. Any audience confronted by a speaker automatically wonders: Who are you? What are your values and beliefs? Why should I trust you? What qualifies you to speak on this subject? What special experience and understanding gives you 'standing' to authoritatively discuss this subject? How willing are you to share your own sometimes painful experiences in order to give authenticity to what you are saying? What 'added value' do *you* bring to the table or the public platform?

Ethos can build a bridge of trust and confidence with another person.

Logos or Reasoning

In Greek, *logos* means reasoning or argument. *Homo sapiens*, the wise and rational human, chooses the optimal outcome based on logical argument. *Logos* is the work of the head. The reasoning process is centred in the left side of the brain.

The framework of rules for building a logical, rational, persuasive and defensible argument is at the heart of Western science, knowledge and institutions. Law is supposed to be rational and logical. Bureaucracy was invented as the rational science of administration. Management consultants apply rational principles to the organisations they study. Western systems of education place overwhelming stress on developing the rational/logical faculties of students. And, in this era of globalisation, even the economy is supposedly managed on the rational principle of the 'level playing field'. Chapter 2, on thinking and organising, devotes itself to *logos* and its practical application in persuasive argument.

Pathos or Passion

Pathos is the feeling or passion you have for your subject. If you don't feel committed to what you say and do, you can't expect others to be committed. *Pathos* has made the transition from Greek to modern usage in English. It means to demonstrate feeling and sympathy or suffering. Passion will do. You don't need to demonstrate suffering for your work, but you do need to show feeling. Passion is the work of the heart. The emotional processing which takes place in the right-hand side of the brain balances the rational processing of the left-hand side.

Australia's dominant Anglo-Celtic culture distrusts passion, almost *with* a passion. The traditional upbringing for boys, in particular, has stressed the need for the ways of the head to dominate the unpredictable wiles of the heart. The experience of European history in this century led observers such as Freud to believe that civilisation depended for its existence on the repression of basic urges and passions.

Yet a life which lacks the yeast of emotion is dull beyond endurance. It is true that emotion starts wars, but emotion is also at the heart of the great refinements of art and culture. Where is music without emotion? Or art? And what about poetry or human communication?

Passion changes the world and it is the people with unshakeable beliefs who make change happen. As the American essayist Emerson remarked, one person with a belief is worth 99 who have only interests. The force of their personality and convictions can influence the emotions and passions of others.

You can't fake passion—people know straight away if you try to. Genuine passion grows out of a deep-seated belief. I am sometimes asked in seminars how someone can express passion when they really don't feel it. Some public servants, for instance, tell me they feel anything but passionate about presenting a routine report. Well, maybe there is no way to be passionate about a routine report. Nevertheless, people can genuinely feel passionate about doing the best job possible on everything they attempt. They can feel a passionate belief in the value of the system in which they are writing their routine report (if they truly believe in it).

I believe that life is too short for confining your passions to home or to your activities outside work. Work takes up too much time for that. If people feel no passion for their work then they can never express passion about it. Maybe they should think about doing something else. That's what John Bell did.

John Bell

My friend, the businessman John Bell (1949–93), embodied real *ethos*, *logos* and *pathos* in his life and the way he communicated. John Bell was the Australian managing director of the Esprit clothing company. He once told me that no one needed to buy another T-shirt, but as a businessman he wanted to weld together his fundamental need to sell more T-shirts with doing good on a wider stage. He wanted to make a difference to the lives of vulnerable young people: unemployed kids, drug-addicted kids, abandoned kids. To do so, he began bringing his heart and soul to work as well as his head.

Late in his short life, John Bell decided that success in business should be measured by more than just profits. He began exploring how he could put more into the community than just fashion items. Those who knew him over many years say his character, wellbeing and peace of mind were transformed by the experience.

In the last year of his life, I worked with John Bell as his communication adviser. I became a sounding board for his ideas on social and environmental issues and how to communicate them. In reality, the relationship went beyond that. Not only were we good friends, but we also became joint mentors for each other.

We had met when I spoke at a business function to launch the Victorian office of a group of non-profit lawyers called the Environmental Defenders. Some time later, he called me and asked whether I would help him to communicate better. He wanted to take his message out into the community. We spent many days working on sharpening his skills. He was hungry for the knowledge. We discussed how to influence different personality styles. What was just the right way to get through to one person or another? How could a person speak with *ethos* or character? What were the most persuasive ways, *logos*, to put together an argument?

What were the best ways to deliver it? What is powerful body language and how do you read the body language of the people who are listening? How could he lead his team of people to feel the same passion, *pathos*, about this mission?

At Esprit, John Bell decided to pursue a strategy of making his company stand for more than just selling clothes. It would be a business with a social conscience. His company would have two bottom lines. Neither the financial bottom line nor the social bottom line would be allowed to over-ride the other.

The Esprit Cares Trust Fund was formed to siphon off a small percentage of the turnover of the company to support community and environmental concerns. The trust gave support to homeless kids, funded the employment of young people beyond the needs of the company, and ran a farm at Taggerty in Victoria as a self-help project for children at risk. Esprit staff could take time off from work each month for voluntary community work.

John Bell was full of plans. He wanted to set up a clothing label of, by and for street kids. He was inspired by the success of the Cross Colours label in Los Angeles where kids from opposing gangs appeared to be working harmoniously on a project to produce a street label. He was confident that Australian street kids also had the potential to set up a street wear line with wide market appeal.

To get his message out, John began arranging a heavy schedule of talks and media appearances, especially on the theme of youth unemployment. He would talk to business breakfasts, lunches and dinners, to community groups and youth groups, to large groups and small. His audiences were often sceptical. They would not be swayed by emotional appeals based on *pathos* alone. Bell worked hard to deliver his message in a framework of solid reasoning or *logos*, arguing his case step by step to its logical conclusion. The frameworks which John Bell and I worked on to organise his thinking are contained in this book.

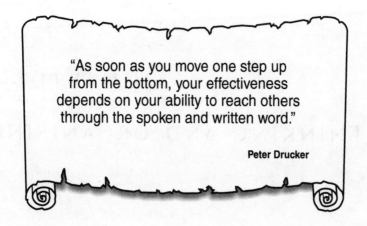

"As soon as you move one step up
from the bottom, your effectiveness
depends on your ability to reach others
through the spoken and written word."

Peter Drucker

He built an evidence bank. A diary/scrapbook was his constant companion. He would paste clippings from newspapers or magazines that interested him or write out a quote he had heard which he thought might be useful some time in the future. He was always turning over in his mind how to say something more effectively or how he might enthuse other business leaders to take up social concerns.

I am often asked the question: Are great communicators born or made? My answer is that, like John Bell, they make themselves through sheer hard work. Some people have natural gifts such as easiness in company and a facility for dealing with others. But that is not enough to make someone effective in the difficult situations of communicating in a business environment in presenting or negotiating with others or in speaking on the media. A friend of mine at the Australian Graduate School of Management, James Carlopio, is fond of saying that communicating with the living is only a little easier than communicating with the dead. He's right.

The purpose of this book is to make communicating with the living a little easier still. Aristotle had it all worked out. Come join me in putting on his thinking cap.

CHAPTER 2

THINKING AND ORGANISING

1 Persuasion in Greece and Rome

2 Five-point plan of persuasion

3 Prototype advertisement using five-point plan of persuasion

4 Using the five-point plan

5 A four-part story: A variation on the five-point plan

6 Which structure is better?

7 Deductive and inductive arguments

8 Cross-cultural communication

9 The key point

10 Constructing an argument: Avoid upside-down thinking

11 Answering questions

12 Question and answer format for presentations

Before they start, they do not know what they are going to say; when they are speaking, they do not know what they are saying; and when they have finished, neither they nor their audience know what they have said.
Winston Churchill, 1912

AT HIS LYCEUM in Athens 2340 years ago, Aristotle taught that the power of logical argument, *logos*, was the most important tool of persuasion, above nobility of sentiment (*ethos*) and polish in style (*pathos*). At the heart of logical argument is the notion of proposition and proof.

To this day, leading-edge business communicators rely on the compelling logical system developed by Aristotle. Whether your communication needs are making a business presentation, writing a letter of proposal, or answering questions in a negotiation or to the media, you need a framework to sharpen your message.

We live in a world where there is too much information and data and too little time to make sense of it. Time has become the scarcest resource as people try to grapple with the uncertainties involved in decision-making. There is rarely enough time to coolly analyse all the information which could have a bearing on the decisions we make. That is why we need excellent systems for organising, analysing and thinking about information.

There is no more important task for executives than being able to condense a mass of information into its essential elements and then create a coherent and persuasive argument to underpin the judgments they make. The structures invented by Aristotle serve this purpose. They impose a framework, or way of thinking about information.

Logical structures are time-saving because they allow you to organise your material quickly into a persuasive argument. It is like learning the shortcuts in a strange city. With this knowledge in your head, you get to your destination in the quickest possible time, with only half the stress.

For example, the former head of a national law firm once told me that, in order to persuade his lawyer colleagues about the merits of something, it was essential to present the idea in a tightly argued logical framework. Lawyers, being the rational creatures that they are, wanted to see the framework before they would buy the contents of the idea inside. He assured me that the same idea, presented without a persuasive conceptual framework, would be rejected out of hand.

Creating a persuasive conceptual framework is also at the heart of what management consultants do. It is no surprise that the McKinsey firm was founded by a group of accountants and lawyers who wanted to apply the analytical and conceptual skills of their disciplines to problem-solving in management. Elite consulting firms bring a number of conceptual models as baggage when they enter a business seeking to solve its problems, but none is more important than the clear-thinking model for logically setting out the framework of the problem and its possible solutions. This chapter reveals the formula which McKinsey and other management consultants use to structure their arguments and present their findings to clients.

Persuasion in Greece and Rome

McKinsey's structure for presenting an argument, shown in detail below, owes a great debt to the thinking taught at Aristotle's Lyceum. Aristotle called the logical structuring of a presentation the 'arrangement'.

The arrangement of an argument would depend on its purpose. Aristotle divided rhetoric into categories dealing with whether or not the audience had to make some judgment. Judicial rhetoric was for persuading a court of law about past events; deliberative rhetoric was persuading an audience about some future action; and demonstrative rhetoric was speeches used on some public occasion to praise or blame. This last category aims to influence or play on the values and beliefs of the audience. A persuasive logical argument doesn't try to change the belief system of the audience, but rather builds on people's existing values.

Contemporary consultants are in the business of deliberative rhetoric—that is, persuading their clients to take some future action—and Aristotle's system for putting a well-organised deliberative case remains the fundamental framework of a persuasive argument. This system has four parts, the most important of which are the proposition and proof:

1 *Exordium*

Introduction. Creating goodwill, putting the audience in a receptive frame of mind. See 'bait' (p.18).

2 *Narratio*

The factual background. Clear, brief and persuasive. This is often deleted in deliberative presentations. See 'problem' (p.18).

3 *Confirmatio or Probatio*

Proof. Usually begins with a proposition. The proof of the case using all available means of persuasion, such as:

    (a)   **showing the benefits that will result;**
    (b)   **appealing to the listener's self-interest.**

Refutes likely objections. Rebuts the case of adversaries. See 'solution' (p.18).

4 *Peroratio*

The speaker reserves his or her strongest appeal for the climax, such as an appeal to self-interest on a higher plane. Aristotle believed there were four elements to this stage:

(a)   Your own material should be amplified.

(b)   The case of an adversary is diminished.

(c)   A summary or recapitulation may also be appropriate at this stage.

(d)   The speech may end by inspiring emotion.

In this century, Winston Churchill, Adolf Hitler, Martin Luther King and others stuck by this creed by ending their speeches on a high emotional pitch. Aristotle suggested a conclusion along the lines of: 'I have spoken, you have heard, you have the facts, judge'.

Five-point Plan of Persuasion

More than 2000 years later, no one has really improved on the principles set out by the Greek teachers of rhetoric. Today, many sophisticated sales pitches made in television advertising follow basically the same framework that was set down by Aristotle and his friends. The following is a classic five-point plan for making a business presentation aimed at persuading an audience. This framework is suitable if you are alerting your audience to a problem or issue on which you want their response. You may be presenting a strategic plan for a business or organisation with a call for specific action. You may be selling ideas or products or services ending with a direct pitch.

1   *Bait (exordium)*: A story or statement which arouses audience interest.

2   *Problem or question (narratio)*: You pose a problem or question that has to be solved or answered.

3   *Solution or answer (confirmatio/probatio)*: You resolve the issues which have been raised.

4 *Pay-off or benefit (peroratio)*: You state specific advantages to each member of the audience of adopting the course of action recommended in the solution or answer.

5 *Call to action (peroratio)*: You state the concrete actions which should follow your presentation.

Watch television for a night or two and you will notice this five-point plan being used as the structure for some advertising. As I am a coffee addict, I will make up an advertisement for a hypothetical Moccafe brand to illustrate how the five-point plan can be used.

Prototype Advertisement Using Five-point Plan of Persuasion

Coffee Advertisement

1 *Bait*: Sexy-looking people wouldn't start their day without coffee. (You identify with this because you see yourself as sexy too and you can't do without coffee in the morning. So your interest is aroused.)

2 *Problem*: The problem or question is: What brand of coffee would sexy people—that is, people who are serious about their coffee—want to be seen with in their kitchen?

3 *Solution*: Moccafe is sexiest for one or two or three reasons:

(a) Taste. It has a special roasting technique.

(b) Reputation. Discerning people buy it.

(c) Price. People know you pay a premium.

4 *Pay-off*: You will be made even sexier by sharing Moccafe or drinking it alone.

5 *Call to action*: Buy Moccafe coffee, of course.

The five-point plan is just as evident in real, and successful, advertisements:

Shell: Air That I Breathe Advertisement

1 *Bait*: Attractive visuals of young people pumping gas. Hollies song on audio track.
2 *Problem*: Over 80 per cent of the lead in the air of our cities comes from car exhaust fumes.
3 *Solution*: So if every car that could only use leaded petrol used Shell Half Lead, our air quality would improve dramatically. Use Shell Half Lead.
4 *Pay-off*: Just as good for your car. Better for the air we all breathe.
5 *Call to action*: Go well. Go Shell.

Evangelists like Billy Graham use the five-point structure in their quest for saving souls at revivalist rallies:

Prototype Billy Graham Presentation Using Five-point Plan

1 *Bait*: I have sinned.
2 *Problem*: We are all sinners.
3 *Solution*: Turn to God.
4 *Pay-off*: You will be saved.
5 *Call to action*: Get down with me and pray.

Using the Five-point Plan

Your business presentations can use the powerful logical arrangement of the five-point plan to be as persuasive as these ads.

The architecture of the five-point plan looks like a kite. It is narrow and sharp at its apex (you talk one-on-one), then widens to addressing the general issues raised by the topic before narrowing again to addressing your audience one-on-one. So it shifts from the specific to the general back to the specific.

Begin your presentation with a bait: get people to be curious and interested in what is to follow. Once this step is achieved, link your bait to a statement of the problem or question which your bait raises. By now the purpose of the presentation should be absolutely clear to the audience. This leads to the detailed resolution of the issue contained in the solution or answer. The pay-off or benefit is a statement of personal advantages to be derived by resolving the issue in the manner suggested. It concludes with a call to action in specific terms.

An aid to helping the audience follow this logical progression is to use the terms contained in the structure as part of the talk:

'The problem is . . .'
'What is the solution?'
'What is the pay-off from adopting this solution?'
'What I am asking you to do is . . .'

Using these terms makes it clear to the audience what stage the talk has reached. Remember that an audience cannot replay your talk to pull the threads of an argument together. They have to be understood on a first hearing or people will switch off.

To avoid confusing your audience, it is important not to revisit an earlier stage of the talk once it has passed. If you are already talking through the solution, avoid saying, 'Another problem is . . .' In fact, if the solution needs qualifying in some way, don't use the term 'problem' again at all, because it will only make the audience think you are returning to an earlier part of the presentation.

This five-point plan is ideal for an impromptu talk as well as a much longer presentation. The art of mastering the impromptu speech is to make your topic manageable by confining your talk to only one aspect of the topic. For example, if the topic is 'rain', reduce the issue to talking about the last time it rained or some other narrowly defined interpretation. It is extremely hard to talk globally about an issue without a lot of thought. Using the five-point plan, however, you can talk about one aspect of an issue with virtually no preparation at all.

To *prepare* your five-point plan, whether the talk is for one minute or one hour, the first stages are to define the problem or question, and your call to action. The call to action is most powerful when it contains concrete actions or tasks which you want the audience to perform. Write down the problem or question and call to action in a few lines. This simple process will help clarify your mind about the task ahead. Of course, in impromptu talks, you may not even enjoy the simple luxury of writing time.

Once you have isolated the problem and your call to action, the next stage of preparation is to work out a solution to your problem. The solution or answer should be no more than three points. How you approach the solution (or 'proof' in Aristotle's logic) will vary according to the problem and the situation in which you are presenting, as we'll find out in the next section. You will then be able to identify the pay-off, or benefit—the individual or personal gain to the audience which will come from adopting your solution. But keep the pay-off quite separate in your presentation structure.

The final stage of preparation is creating a bait. This is prepared last but presented first. It is the stage of preparation which people attending my seminars on communication have most trouble grappling with. What makes a good bait? As the term implies, like the angler hooking the fish, you want to hook your audience with the bait. The most important element of the bait is that it is connected to the problem or question which is to follow.

The best baits are stories from personal experience which illustrate a microcosm of the problem. Personal stories and anecdotes work well because they are usually strongly felt by the speaker and are relatively easy to remember in the telling. Personal anecdotes help the audience to identify with the speaker and get to know their character. These stories also have the advantage of helping to relax the speaker in the difficult opening stage of the presentation. Metaphors make excellent baits. (A whole section of the book on the creation of metaphors follows in Chapter 3.) A powerful or shocking statistic can be a successful bait. But whatever the bait is, its object is to make the audience listen with avid curiosity to what follows.

The following example shows the five-point plan being used in a short presentation. The topic is, 'Should Australia become a republic?' See if you can follow the 'kite' of the five-point plan, moving from the specific to the general argument to the specific call to action.

Prototype Five-point Plan Speech on an Australian Republic

1 Bait

Symbols are important. People still choose to marry today because it is a symbolic as well as a legal recognition of their relationship. That is why I married. Many families have special affectionate names for their children as symbols of the bonds which exist in a family. That is why we have a special family name for our daughter. As Australians, you and I also value the symbols which tie us together and identify our democracy. The flag and anthem are two such symbols.

Note: Personal references in the bait reveal something of the speaker's character or ethos. The symbols are individual and family-specific first, moving to general and national in scope at the end.

2 Problem or question

The problem is that one of our key national symbols—the position of our head of state—is no longer appropriate to the sort of mature nation that we now are. The head of state is the symbolic personification of our nationhood. Did you know there is no mention of the prime minister or cabinet in our constitution? The only person mentioned in our constitution is the Queen's representative, the governor-general. It is quite absurd to look to Buckingham Palace as the centre of Australian identity as we approach the second century of our nationhood.

Note: The bait is linked to the problem directly through the discussion of symbols in both.

3 Solution or answer

The move to a republic has both rational and emotional appeal.

Note: The solution contains opportunities for detailed arguments.

There are three reasons for this. First, Australia's democracy is secure and does not need ties to Britain to safeguard it. Second, Australia's national identity now reflects the multicultural origins of our population. Our links to British heritage have declined as the ethnic makeup of the country has changed. Third, Australia and Britain are now enmeshed in their own regions, Australia in

Asia and the Pacific and Britain in Europe through its membership of the EU.

Note: The discussion of the solution allows for spelling out the key arguments in detail.

4 *Pay-off*

The benefit to all of us from changing the constitution is that we will feel proud that our national symbols are in line with modern reality. All of us want to live in a truly contemporary society, not one where we are forced to cringe when explaining our national institutions to others. Imagine the embarrassment of having to explain to your foreign friends why the British monarch opened the Sydney Olympic Games. You will be saved such embarrassment only if Australia moves quickly to change its constitution.

Note: Shift from the general in the solution to the specific in the pay-off. Also note final linking sentence to the call for action which follows.

5 *Call to action*

Support Australia becoming a republic so that the Olympic Games in 2000 is opened by an Australian head of state. You can contribute to the momentum for change by joining the Australian Republican Movement.

Note: Call to action always contains concrete steps.

A Four-part Story: A Variation on the Five-point Plan

A variation of the five-point plan is contained in the structure favoured by management consultants McKinsey and Co. Helen

Nugent, a long-serving partner at McKinsey before joining Westpac as head of strategy, told me that learning to apply this corporate structure was the most important thing that she had learned at McKinsey. The structure is particularly effective in presentations where the main purpose is identifying a problem and then solving it. It follows the oldest story-telling routine in history.

The Structure of a Four-part Story

1 *Situation*

Briefly tell the audience things they already know which sum up the state of the business, the market, or whatever issue is the focus of the presentation. The situation is designed to be a brief synopsis or overview of conditions which are well known to the audience. Do not create disagreement at this stage.

2 *Complication*

Identify a complication or problem which threatens the viability of the status quo outlined in the situation. This may take the form of changing market conditions, a slowdown in growth or the entry of new competitors, technological change or issues in industrial relations.

The complication may answer one of the following questions: What's changed? What's happened? What's new? What's different now? What's upset the way things were? What's gone wrong?

3 *Question*

The problem identified in the complication leads to the formation of a question. For example: What can be done? What choices do we have? How can we succeed? How do we proceed?

4 *Answer*

The answer or hypothesis takes up the great bulk of the presentation and is a detailed response to the issue raised by the
question.

This classic story-telling formula is commonly used by authors
and creators writing books and making movies. Consider an
example from ABC Television's great success story for children,
Bananas in Pyjamas.

Bananas in Pyjamas Four-part Story Line

1 *Situation*

The bananas, B1 and B2, are having a birthday. They are planning
a party for themselves but don't intend to tell their neighbourhood
friends, the teddies, until the last minute.

2 *Complication*

The teddies, unaware of the bananas' plans, are organising their
own surprise birthday party for the bananas.

3 *Question*

What will happen as the two parties are planned secretly?

4 *Answer*

A great deal of confusion results, but all ends happily with the
bananas and teddies sharing the goodies they each purchased for
their respective parties.

Using the Four-part Story in Letters of Proposal

A house rule at McKinsey and Co is that all letters of proposal sent from the organisation must be set out using the four-part story. The great strength of using this structure for such letters is that it places issues in the mind of the client in the first three paragraphs of the letter. Take the following example:

Letter to potential client from a law firm.

1 *Situation*

You may be happily married now.

2 *Complication*

But the sad fact is that one-third of marriages end in divorce. You should not ignore reality and the odds you face.

3 *Question*

What prudent and proactive steps should you take to be well prepared in case the worst happens?

4 *Answer*

Begin saving.

Note: The answer should set out a number of steps to be taken.

Which Structure is Better?

The five-point plan is an excellent structure for making a sales presentation where you are asking the audience to buy a product

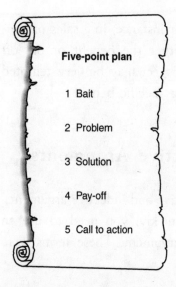
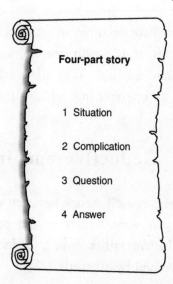

Five-point plan

1 Bait

2 Problem

3 Solution

4 Pay-off

5 Call to action

Four-part story

1 Situation

2 Complication

3 Question

4 Answer

Figure 2.1 Structures

or service. The bait is designed to hook the audience's interest and create a high level of involvement. The call to action is a specific request to buy. The simplicity and logic of this structure also makes it easy to design a speedy presentation, such as in an impromptu situation.

The four-part story, on the other hand, is ideal for a spoken or written report to a client. It assumes that not much effort is required to gain the interest of the audience in the subject. It is very focused on the key question–answer nexus. McKinsey and Co advise their consultants to get to the answer stage within one minute. They assume that their high-level audiences will be impatient to get to the point. Delay beyond one minute risks presenting to an audience which is no longer giving its full attention.

There is no absolute rule about which structure will suit individual purposes. The best advice is to think through each situation and decide which is appropriate for the occasion. You can also massage the structures. Try changing the order to see if your case becomes more forceful. For instance, in a sales presentation, it is worth considering whether the benefit or pay-off should go first. After all, a sales prospect may be very tempted by an opening line which promises a specific benefit.

Deductive and Inductive Arguments

There is a difference between deductive and inductive arguments. If you want to get to the point quickly, you need to use an inductive rather than a deductive argument. These terms were invented by Aristotle.

Deductive Argument

Deductive arguments are a step-by-step process of building a conclusion based on laying out all the premises. The classic example used of a deductive argument is 'All men are mortal. Socrates is a man. Therefore Socrates is mortal.' The argument begins with a major premise. It is followed by a minor premise which is linked to the first. By deduction, you then draw a conclusion. The test of a deductive argument is whether the conclusion is true or false. If your audience needs the assurance of a slowly paced argument which cautiously builds agreement about all the steps before leaping to a conclusion, then a deductive argument is best. However, such an argument can run off the rails before you get to the conclusion if there is disagreement with one of your premises.

Inductive Argument

An inductive argument works the other way. It usually flows away from your conclusion. An inductive argument is a generalisation which is assumed to apply to and support the propositions which flow from it. The test of an inductive argument is whether the evidence supporting the conclusion is strong or weak. The propositions which flow from an inductive argument are sometimes called the legs. Take the following inductive argument. 'Taxation reform will strengthen Australia's competitiveness.' The legs of the argument which flow from this proposition are:

1 Reform will reduce the costs of doing business.
2 Reform will shift the burden from direct to indirect tax and is an incentive to work.
3 Reform will attract foreign investment in some sectors.

The test of the argument that 'tax reform will strengthen Australia's competitiveness' therefore lies in the strength or weakness of the three legs which support the case. These legs are always put after the generalisation.

Inductive arguments are more creative and powerful than deductive ones because they move beyond established facts. Their proofs are looser and their conclusions can be more speculative and dynamic. We must use our own judgment to decide whether the evidence strongly supports the conclusion. On the other hand, deductive arguments are conservative. The true/false test mostly means a deductive conclusion is locked into things we know for sure. Most of the things that are worthwhile and interesting to think about—like the best organisational structure for your business—lie beyond the banalities of what we know for sure! Although we might accept that Socrates is mortal, where does that conclusion take us? Not very far, because it is so plainly obvious! When you are analysing your business or even your love life, it is far more dynamic to take a look beyond what is known for certain.

If your audience is ready to be fast tracked to hear your general conclusion and then listen to the supporting evidence, go for an inductive argument. If you are presenting in a business climate where time is short and there is agreement about the basic issues, always argue inductively.

Cross-cultural Communication

As Western business becomes increasingly enmeshed in the Asia-Pacific region, recognition needs to be given to the cultural differences of other societies.

Professors at some Australian universities complain that their Asian students are reluctant to make a central point in their essays, project reports and oral presentations. These Asian students are merely conforming, however, to their own cultural style in which, in some situations, the audience is left to draw its own conclusions about the message of a presentation.

Business is done differently in Asia. It operates by different norms. Choosing a business partner is rarely based on a competitive pitch or presentation alone, but involves a long process of relationship-building. The relationship between the parties may be developed at first through personal contacts and over time is nurtured through social engagements, even a game of golf.

In some Asian societies, making a skilful business presentation requires mastering the indirect approach. Speakers can talk around the point, reaching what the Japanese call a *ketsu*, or non-conclusion, rather than talking to the point. It illustrates the different place of business presentations in Asian societies.

The concept of 'face' is also an important element in the developing relationship. It is embarrassing in many Asian societies to say 'no'. A traditional Western-style presentation usually demands a 'yes' or 'no' answer by the client. Creating such a clear-cut choice, while perfectly acceptable at 'home', can seem insensitive in an Asian context.

Understanding the authority structure of an Asian business is another prerequisite to marketing success. In a Western business setting, presenters usually start with the gung-ho assumption that their task is to persuade the audience. In the traditional Asian business setting, however, formal authority tends to rest on one pair of shoulders only. The head of the group is deferred to with great respect by other members of the organisation. In this environment, a presenter doesn't so much need to 'win' the argument with the group, but gain the respect of its most senior member.

The Key Point

Being able to pick the key point in your case is central to persuasive speaking and writing in the law, business and politics.

Leading QC Tom Hughes shed light on the art of persuasiveness when he said in a portrait article in the *Weekend Australian* that he believed being successful in the modern law requires a difficult combination of being brief but thorough at the same time. The essence of winning in court is to pick the real point of the case and not flog the ones which have no legs.

James Carville, Bill Clinton's presidential campaign director in 1992, hung a poster in the Little Rock headquarters which said 'The Economy, Stupid', a play on the old saying, 'Keep it simple, stupid'. It was a sharp daily reminder that the focus of the year-long campaign should not drift away from one message. The opinion polls were showing that Clinton's strongest point was the weak economic state of the United States under George Bush. Years later, an article on James Carville in *Vanity Fair* remarked that it required no act of genius to pick Bush's weak point.

Carville's genius was to impose the discipline of sticking to one point when there were virtually daily opportunities for distractions into second-order issues.

Just as picking the point of the case is vital, it is also crucial not to have too many points. Most people who find themselves speaking as experts on a subject really know what they are talking about. It becomes a constant temptation for them to present too many points of detail. The problem is that the detail is usually lost on the audience. As Voltaire said, the easiest way to bore someone to death is to tell them everything you know about a subject.

Constructing an Argument: Avoid Upside-down Thinking

Many people make the mistake of presenting their argument from the wrong end. They argue upside down. It's what they were taught at school and university. An upside-down argument begins by laying out all the premises of the case and then reaching a conclusion. The problem with arguing upside-down is that you tempt your audience to turn off before you reach your main points and conclusion. This sort of method requires real patience on the part of the listener. Certainly, you finally reach your conclusion, but will the audience stay the course of the argument with you?

Upside-down presentations look like an inverted triangle, where the base becomes the apex. Your argument flows downwards towards a conclusion.

Right-side-up presentations begin with the conclusion or the key idea of the argument. The supporting case is the detail which occupies the space beneath. The great virtue of right-side-up presenting is that you get to the point right away. Your audience can then see the relationship between the conclusion and the parts of your argument as you develop them. At McKinsey they call this right-side-up thinking the *pyramid principle*. The point always comes first, at the apex of the pyramid.

Answering Questions

It is not enough to make an effective presentation if you then fall down on answering questions. After all, persuasive presentations identify and address the underlying or key questions in the minds of the audience. The most effective method of dealing with questions asked at the end of your presentation is to anticipate them. Naturally, the same rules apply in answering questions from a journalist in a media interview. I'll give more consideration to this in Chapter 7.

As part of your business preparation, write out the most likely questions you will be asked and the answers you would give. In particular, give attention to the questions you would least like to be asked.

Format for Effective Answering

You can follow a simple format for giving effective answers to questions.

1 *Point*

This is the one point or statement you want to make in reply to the question.

2 *Reason*

This is the one supporting argument for the point. After stating your point, you can begin Part 2 by saying, 'That's because . . .' or 'The reason is . . .'

3 *Example*

This is the example or brief story which illustrates the point you have made.

In reality, it is not easy to think of this structure as you spontaneously respond to questions. However, if you develop the habit of mind of thinking about answering questions in this way before you face a live audience, you will create the discipline of sticking closely enough to this structure.

Illustration of Point, Reason, Example Answering Structure

Question:	How do you effectively answer questions?
Answer:	Stick to the structure—point, reason, example [point]. That's because it is spare and logical [reason]. For example, too many people never come to the point when answering questions. You know Harry. He is lost in the wilderness when he answers a question. If you are trying to follow him, you get lost too [example].

Question and Answer Format for Presentations

As an alternative to the five-point plan and four-part story, the question and answer format is a powerful presentation structure. Its strength is that it addresses the questions that are in the mind of the audience.

Making this format work means anticipating the real questions in the minds of your audience.

Example: Question and Answer Format in Presentation

I believe the five key questions which you as decision-makers must answer in your own minds are the following:

1 What are your key needs in purchasing a new system?
2 Which proposal most closely fits your needs?
3 Does your preferred provider fit your budgetary parameters?
4 How would the new system be installed?
5 What continuing service would be provided to support the new system?

In today's presentation, I will try to answer the questions in your mind and explain how our system meets your needs.

The example identifies five questions in the mind of the client. The presentation will then be devoted to answering those questions. Blending this question and answer format with the five-point plan, you may set out your presentation as follows:

Bait
Question 1. Answer. Benefit.
Question 2. Answer. Benefit.
Question 3. Answer. Benefit.
Question 4. Answer. Benefit.
Question 5. Answer. Benefit.
Call to action

CHAPTER 3

PERSUASIVE LANGUAGE

1 Switching on the whole brain
2 How the brain processes information
3 The senses: Visual, auditory, kinesthetic
4 Creating word pictures
5 Metaphor and Aristotle
6 Sources of metaphor
7 Seven steps for creating metaphors and images
8 Humour
9 Storytelling
10 Being wholly persuasive

I hear and I forget. I see and I remember. I do and I understand.
Attributed to Confucius

In truth, the ideas and images in men's minds are the invisible powers that constantly govern them.
John Locke

SOME PEOPLE HAVE a way with words. They make language come alive. Their words spit and boil or caress you like a sea breeze. Word pictures come naturally to them. Other people bore you with their words. They use thousands of words when a few would do. They talk in jargon or arid bureaucratese.

Their images are clichéd or non-existent. Sadly, most people in business talk in a dull way rather than with bright, animated language.

One person inspires and persuades you; another sends you to sleep. One makes you effortlessly remember what they say; another just makes you want to forget. When one person speaks, you don't notice the time passing. When the other speaks, you keep looking at your watch and daydream about more pleasant things.

Developing persuasive language powers is one technique which can make you a powerful communicator. There are just a few principles involved. In this section, the focus is on how you can say something in such a way as to make your audience actually want to remember it. Aristotle called this the 'style' of rhetoric— the language of persuasion.

People quickly forget nearly everything that is said to them. This is hardly surprising given the constant demands on their attention. They are bombarded by thousands of messages every day. So if you want your message to be remembered in this world of information overload and forgetfulness, you haven't many options. One is to repeat yourself endlessly, which can become tiresome both for the speaker and the audience. Another is to use words which act like a stamp on people's memories. Once there, the words stick like a spider's prey in a web. They become memory hooks. But before we get to that point, it is useful to know more about how people think and process information.

Switching on the Whole Brain

To find the key to how people think it is necessary to get inside their heads. More than half a century ago, Rudyard Kipling wrote a poem 'The Two-sided Man'.

I would go without shirt or shoe,
Friend, tobacco or bread,
Sooner than lose for a minute the two
Separate sides of my head!

Dr Roger Sperry began conducting research into the operation of the brain in the 1950s and 1960s. Sperry, later awarded the Nobel Prize for his work, found that our brains have two separate modes of thinking—verbal and non-verbal. (The notion that there are two parts to our brains—and to our natures—the opposing while complementary forces of yin and yang, has in fact been around for thousands of years.) He carried out 'split-brain studies', as they have become known, on patients suffering severe epilepsy. The communication pathways between the left and right hemispheres of the brain were severed in an attempt to control seizures and the surgery had the desired result for the patients. The fits were controlled while their physical coordination was unaffected. In further studies, Sperry and his team found that the two halves of the brain continued to function independently after the connecting cable was severed. That cable, made up of millions of fibres, acted only to integrate the two modes of thinking.

The left hemisphere of the brain is analytical. The right hemisphere of the brain is creative. This division is sometimes reversed for left-handers. Maths, numbers, logic, sequence, judgment and speech are features which are at home in the left brain. Painting, art, music, imagination, creativity and daydreaming are at home in the right brain.

To communicate an idea effectively, you must use both the left and right sides of your brain in order to connect with both sides of the listener's brain. Not many of us do this. As a result, few people really reach their persuasive potential when communicating with others. As I once read, 'while half a brain is better

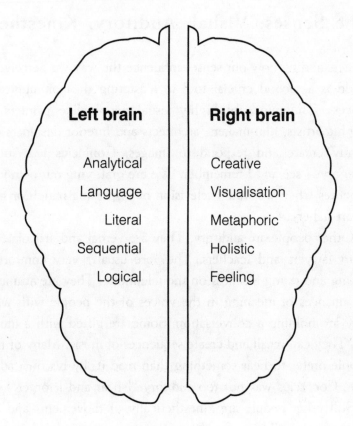

Figure 3.1 How the brain processes information

than none, a whole brain would be better'. The right brain isn't a spare tyre; it has the same level of importance as the left brain. Think about a motorbike—if you leave one tyre flat, you won't make the same progress as with both tyres working.

Too many speakers, media performers and negotiators use language entirely sourced and manufactured in their left brain. It is the dry language of logic and analysis. On the other hand, persuasive communicators speak with both the logical/analytical powers of the left brain and the creative, visual and metaphoric powers sourced in the right brain.

The Senses: Visual, Auditory, Kinesthetic

Understanding how our senses influence the way we perceive the world is a second crucial tool in mastering the communication process. The minds of highly visual people like painters and graphic artists, film-makers, architects and interior designers constantly create and respond to images. Confucius was in this category: 'I see and I remember.' We are gratifying our own visual appetites when we watch television or a sporting match or go to an art gallery.

Other people are auditory. They are verbal and articulate like smart lawyers and teachers. They are usually very comfortable talking and doing business on the telephone. They are attuned to the nuances of meaning in the voices of the people with whom they are holding a conversation. Some are gifted with a musical ear. They can recall and create sequences of music. Many of these people prefer to hear something than read it. By his own admission, Confucius was not too auditory: 'I hear and I forget.'

Still other people are kinesthetically or movement- and feeling-oriented. They are 'hands on' people who are most comfortable learning through doing. They are carpenters and builders and mechanics, or maybe dancers and athletes. Many kinesthetics are also skilled at observing the emotional states of other people. Others, like wine-tasters and food experts, are finely attuned to smell (olfactory) and taste (gustatory) senses too. (Writer Patrick Suskind brings the much neglected sense of smell alive in the fine novel *Perfume*, set in the 'sweaty, fetid eighteenth century' in which the main character has the finest nose in Paris and no personal odour.)

Neurolinguistic programming (NLP) is the study of how the various sensory channels of communication influence the perception and learning process. It looks at the relationship between thinking, language and behaviour. Experts in NLP and accelerated learning make use of the link between each of the five senses or channels of communication and the learning process. Visually oriented people will learn faster and more effectively through seeing rather than hearing or doing. Auditory learners respond best to spoken stimulus. Kinesthetic people are hands-on learners who will benefit most from practical exercises. Maybe Confucius was mostly kinesthetic: 'I do and I understand.'

'I see what you mean,' says someone who may be visually channelled. 'I like what I hear,' says the auditorily channelled. 'It feels right,' says the kinesthetically oriented person.

Studies by the originators of NLP, the linguist John Grinder and computer programmer Richard Bandler, show that the population is divided into visual, auditory and kinesthetic in the ratio of visual 40 per cent, auditory 40 per cent, kinesthetic 20 per cent.

A Playful and Suggestive List of Sensory Stimuli

These stimuli show that we can easily switch in to all sensory channels. The mere sight of the words and a moment's reflection can bring the image or sound or touch or smell or taste alive.

Visual

Sunrise and sunset
Saddam Hussein
Madonna
A patchwork of fields from
  an aircraft
Children at Christmas
Uluru (Ayers Rock)

Auditory/Sound

Beethoven's Fifth Symphony
  (opening)
Fingernails down a
  blackboard
Sirens
Rain on a tin roof
A yacht at its mooring

The sound of gravel beneath
a car wheel

Kinesthetic/Touch

Oppressive heat/
humidity
Feet on hot sand
Sweaty palms
Walking on a log
Pins and needles
Seaweed when swimming
at a beach
Butterflies in your stomach

Olfactory/Smell

The nose of a Coonawarra
red wine
Freshly cut grass
Tarred roads after rain on a
hot summer's day
Dampness in a cupboard
Suntan oil
A bakery

Gustatory/Taste

A kiss
Freshly brewed coffee

Exciting the sensory imagination of a listener is a key to placing ideas in the long-term memory. Ideas expressed in sensory language, a right-brain activity, become embedded in the listener's memory and can be more easily retrieved than facts. I express this concept in the formula:

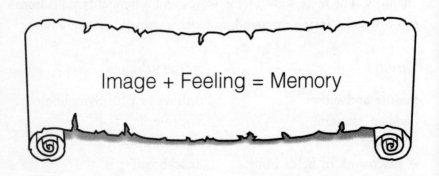

Image + Feeling = Memory

Where the term image means any idea or story expressed in sensory language and feeling is the emotion which the story evokes.

Creating Word Pictures

So what does a persuasive communicator do with this knowledge about how people respond to the different sensory channels? Use it!

Educators design their programs to accommodate the different learning styles of each type. In creating a seminar, I give careful consideration to how to program according to the three key sensory channels—visual, auditory and kinesthetic. I plan to include in each session a range of stimuli including visual and video, sound and hands-on practical work.

When preparing a written presentation, I deliberately seek to include references to the five sensory channels. For example, the following is an excerpt from a speech I made at the tenth anniversary dinner held to mark the High Court's decision to protect Tasmania's Franklin River from hydro-electric development.

Tonight the Franklin runs free. The Franklin is free. Tonight the stars stretch across the heavens above a cold, wild river. (*visual*) If we dipped our hands into that wild river, we would shiver with its cold. (*kinesthetic*)

Tonight perhaps a frost is clinging to the Huon pines as they lean over the splashing rapids of the upper river . . . and the long stretches of the low, broad river. (*visual*) Tonight there is thunder—like there is every night—as the river is channelled through the Churn and the Cauldron. (*auditory*)

Tonight the tea-coloured river is sluicing through Thunder Rush. (*visual and auditory*) Tonight the moon may be casting its deep shadow across the mighty precipice of the

Great Ravine. (*visual*) Tonight the river is rising and falling—as it has done for millions of years. (*visual*)

Tonight we can smell its freedom. (*olfactory*) We can taste
its freedom too. (*gustatory*)

I was confident that each of these sentences would provoke a
sensory stimulus (I call it an 'image' for short) and an emotion in
the audience. The passage was carefully engineered to touch on
each of the five sensory channels. Try using this technique
yourself, not just at an after-dinner occasion, but each time you
want to provoke an emotional response in a business setting.

Metaphor and Aristotle

Of all the devices used to enrich language, metaphor is the most
powerful. Aristotle said: 'The most important thing by far is to
have a command of metaphor. For this is the only one that cannot
be learned from anyone else, and is a sign of natural genius, as
to be good at metaphor is to perceive resemblances . . . It gives
clearness, charm and distinction to style.' Aristotle understood that
powerful metaphors come from sensory language. In *On Rhetoric*,
he observed that 'metaphor is judged not only by its fit to the
thing signified, but also by its sound or by the appeal it makes
to the eye or some other sense'.

Metaphor means the process of transferring or carrying over.
When you create a metaphor, you carry meaning across from one
thing to another, and the power to do this exists in the right side
of the brain, the seat of the imagination. Creating metaphors turns
language into art by enabling people to see things in new ways,
by pointing to an unexpected resemblance or relationship between
things. When we create a metaphor, we are using language for

its real purpose: to express meaning. We are entering the realm of the imagination.

Few of us have the eye and drafting skills to paint or the ear to write music, but we all have the building blocks in our heads to create metaphoric meaning. As the social anthropologist Claude Levi-Strauss said: 'Metaphor, far from being a decoration that is added to language, purifies it and restores it to its original meaning.'

Metaphors make meaning. If you create a metaphor, you are showing people how to see things in a fresh way. The metaphoric stories of mythology shaped and terrified the ancient world. Metaphoric religious texts remain a dominant influence thousands of years after they were written. Last century, economist Adam Smith invented the 'invisible hand' to assure us that there was redemption in the free market system as it directed the selfish acts of individuals, as if by an 'invisible hand', into socially responsible paths. In postwar Europe, Winston Churchill lamented that 'an iron curtain has descended across the continent'.

As a young schoolboy, I was impressed by the 'domino theory', which implied that if one country fell to communism, adjoining countries would topple in a domino effect.

In this ecological era, we are all aboard 'spaceship earth'. We can connect with each other through the 'information superhighway'. We live in a society where women hit their heads against 'the glass ceiling' as they are prevented from achieving success by invisible barriers.

Metaphors burn imprints into the mind. They narrow the focus of a listener's attention to what the speaker wants them to see. Take an example cited by Catherine Lumby in the *Sydney Morning Herald*. Under the headline 'Good girls do get raped', she wrote:

A young Sydney barrister, discussing the recent Victorian case—the Hakopian case—in which a man received a lighter

sentence for raping a prostitute, offered the following analogy: raping a prostitute, he said, was like stealing a car left
in the middle of George Street with its doors unlocked and
the key in the ignition.

Half an hour after our conversation, I had forgotten the
legal subtleties he urged upon me. His analogy, on the other
hand, was bright in my mind. It told me more, after all,
about attitudes women face in our criminal justice system
than hours of jurisprudential debate.

Although Lumby disagreed with it, the analogy was bright in her
mind. That is what metaphor does. It both evokes imagery and
feeling which are the keys to storing information in the long-term
memory.

Biblical Metaphor

The greatest texts in our literature are rich in metaphor. The Old
Testament of the Bible contains such expressions as 'an eye for
an eye, a tooth for a tooth', at once literal and metaphoric in
meaning. Some Christians treat the Bible as a literal text, while
for others it is an extended metaphor, but whatever beliefs people
hold, the Bible is a phenomenal source of metaphor in modern
language.

But of the tree of the knowledge of good and evil, thou
shalt not eat it.

Genesis 2:17

But his wife looked back from behind him and she became
a pillar of salt.

Genesis 19:26

A land flowing with milk and honey.

Exodus 3:8

Follow me, and I will make you fishers of men.

Matthew 4:19

It is easier for a camel to go through the eye of a needle, than for a rich man to enter the kingdom of God.

Matthew 19:24

Metaphoric Shakespeare

Next to the Bible, the great bard's work is the richest source of metaphor in our literature.

This royal throne of kings, this sceptred isle,
This earth of majesty, this seat of Mars,
This other Eden, demi-paradise,
This fortress built by nature for herself
Against infection and the hand of war,
This happy breed of men, this little world,
This precious stone set in the silver sea,
Which serves it in the office of a wall,
Or as a moat defensive to a house,
Against the envy of less happier lands,
This blessed plot, this earth, this realm, this England.

Richard II

How sharper than a serpent's tooth it is
To have a thankless child.

King Lear

But soft! What light through yonder window breaks?
It is the East, and Juliet is the sun!
Arise, fair sun, and kill the envious moon,
Who is already sick and pale with grief.

Romeo and Juliet

The winter of our discontent.

Richard III

Metaphor in Politics: The Banana Republic

In May 1986, Paul Keating, then Treasurer of Australia, was taking
part in a talkback radio program. In the course of a lengthy
conversation, he said:

> We must let Australians know truthfully, honestly, earn-
> estly, just what sort of international hole Australia is in. If
> this government cannot get the adjustment, get manufactur-
> ing going again and keep moderate wage outcomes and a
> sensible economic policy, then Australia is basically done
> for. We will just end up being a third rate economy . . .
> a banana republic.

The banana republic image was soon flashed on the dealing
screens of the foreign exchange jockeys. In the course of the next
24 hours, the Australian dollar traded through a four-cent range,
falling four cents before recovering three cents. The banana
republic comment had seismic political consequences. As Paul
Kelly wrote in his book, *The End of Certainty*, 'Keating's remark was
inadvertent but it became a psychological pivot'. It was quite an
achievement for a chance remark. It contained neither facts nor
figures. It was simply an image—a metaphor. It demonstrated, in

the terms of the old cliché, that a picture is worth a thousand words. Or, in the words of the rock song, 'Every picture tells a story, don't it.'

Years later, the Liberals finally scored off Keating with the invention of the highly effective image, 'five minutes of economic sunshine'. This phrase hurt Labor badly.

The hapless Treasurer, Ralph Willis, responded that there had been a record period of positive economic growth, as measured by quarterly figures from the Australian Bureau of Statistics. But the economic sunshine metaphor worked because it connected with what people were really feeling. The official figures may have told one story, but it was not what large sections of the community actually felt in the gut. Labor made things worse for itself by becoming obsessed with trying to defeat an image with the weight of numbers.

Metaphor in Business and Economics

As the Tokyo stockmarket fell precipitously in 1995, Cathy Mitsui, a market analyst with Goldman Sachs, said: 'It seems everybody is afraid to catch a falling knife.' Imagery and metaphor play a powerful role in explaining business and economic concepts. In fact, the more abstruse the subject, the greater the role metaphors can have in clarifying ideas.

The 1980s was the era of swashbuckling corporate takeovers and the business language and metaphors of the time reflected the mood. Testosterone-soaked young masters of the universe sought to make their millions from wheeling and dealing. Vulnerable companies would send 'poison pills' to 'predatory shareholders' or buy them off with 'greenmail'. 'White knights' would charge to the rescue of ailing companies to fend off the 'corporate raiders'. 'Golden parachutes' would be strapped on by dumped executives who sought a 'soft landing'.

When corporations engage in cut-throat competition for survival or market share, doing business is akin to war. Battle and military strategy as metaphor have a long history. The current popularity in the business literature of the 2000-year-old writings of the Chinese military philosopher and strategist Sun Tsu is a testament to the enduring power of a good war metaphor. Sun Tsu is deeply Taoist in his philosophy, with dictums like 'To win without fighting is best'. He was a warrior philosopher charged with preparing and conducting wars, but his insights are metaphors for managing human relations, psychology, conflict resolution and business strategy.

Sources of Metaphor

Effective metaphors do not emerge just because you want one. Where do the best images and metaphor come from? They can come from anywhere, but some patterns emerge in the choices people make. Research by John Clancy in his book *The Invisible Powers: The Language of Business* found that the six most commonly used metaphors are a journey, machine, organism, war, game and society.

Journeys have been the most enduring source of imagery, particularly sea voyages. For example, Lee Iacocca spoke of himself 'jumping ship' to Chrysler, being in 'uncharted waters' and sailing on a 'sinking ship'. Children are also connected at a young age to the metaphors of travel. In past years, fables such as *The Canterbury Tales*, *Pilgrim's Progress* and *Gulliver's Travels* provided the connection, but in our times *The Wizard of Oz* and science fiction have gone a long way towards replacing these old stories with new metaphors.

Economic change bears on the sorts of images which gain currency. For instance, the industrial age spawned the metaphoric use of machinery in literature and speech. About 1770, Josiah Wedgwood (the creator of the porcelain tradition which bears his name), who was a crusader for improving the working conditions of his employees, compared society with a machine.

The ruling ideas of an era also become a source of metaphor. A century later, social Darwinism imagery was in its heyday of use by business. It fitted the robber baron era of *laissez faire* and survival of the fittest. In the cybernetic age of systems theory, game metaphors were the rage. Now, in this ecological age, business as an organism is one of the most frequently cited images.

Animal behaviour is a regular source of imagery. Many people affectionately call their cherished loved ones possum or pussycat. War heroes are tigers and lions. Economist John Maynard Keynes wrote of the 'animal spirits' unleashed by the marketplace. Animals were also a favourite source of imagery for Winston Churchill. Speaking of appeasement policies by European nations towards Hitler's Germany, he said: 'Each one hopes that if he feeds the crocodile enough, that the crocodile will eat him last. All hope that the storm will pass before their turn comes to be devoured.' Churchill once summed up his Labour successor Clement Attlee as 'a sheep in sheep's clothing'.

Like war, sport embodies a contest, see-sawing fortunes, winners and losers, the will to win, courage and heroism, grace under pressure, drama, tenacity and defiance against odds.

Metaphors can be drawn from nature to illustrate growth, the life cycle, wonder and mystery, beauty and awe, vastness and microscopic detail, simplicity and complexity, power and mastery over human forces, purpose or randomness, chaos, survival of the fittest, interdependence and the relationships between things.

Our bodies offer themselves as rich pickings for metaphoric meaning. The brain, eyes, ears, nose, heart, arms, hands, fingers, legs, feet, lungs, liver, kidneys and so on all suggest images we can use.

Seven Steps for Creating Metaphor and Images

1 Put yourself in a receptive frame of mind—try going for a peaceful walk or playing music.
2 Brainstorm images—stories from journeys, sport, nature, the human body, machines and animals are among the best sources of metaphor.
3 Choose a simple image to which people can relate.
4 Write down the reasons why your image explains the message you want to send.
5 Develop your image by focusing on a few details of the picture.
6 Avoid clichés and ponder whether your image is fresh enough to have an effect.
7 Rehearse the metaphor aloud.

Humour

Humour, like metaphor, makes us see the world differently. Aristotle advised that arguments were made more persuasive when seasoned by the salt of wit. Cicero of Rome (106–43 BC) was regarded as the greatest orator of his era and 58 of his major speeches have survived. He wrote about the role of humour in his work *On the Orator*:

> It secures good will by whom it is aroused, or because all admire the sharpness inherent often in a single word, especially in replying to criticism and sometimes in attacking; and most of all because it softens and relaxes seriousness and tension and by laughter often dissolves troublesome matters which could not easily be disposed of by arguments.

Humour connects speaker and audience. It creates real communication because the audience actively responds to the speaker through laughter. Humour transforms the emotional state of the audience.

When do you use humour? Pretty much any time. It is a renowned ice-breaker or bait to begin the most serious of talks. The British prime minister, Tony Blair, routinely begins his public speeches with amusing stories. Many of these work well because they take the 'mickey', indicating that he doesn't view himself too seriously. In his early days as prime minister he would remark: 'I'm still at the stage that, when I hear the prime minister is here, I start looking around.'

On some occasions, such as speaking after dinner or at a celebration, being humorous is the speaker's main task. In these situations, everyone wants to be amused. The business environment is not always so funny. However, don't be discouraged. Audiences all appreciate humour if it does not take too much time or distract from the main business at hand. Ironically, it is at times when humour is least expected, such as at sorrowful occasions like a funeral, that it can bring greatest release.

Everyone can be humorous, but not everyone can tell jokes. There is an important difference between the two and if you are not good at joke telling, don't try to do it. Jokers need to be raconteurs, people skilled at recounting amusing stories and anecdotes. The joke usually lies in the hidden or unexpected meaning or twist of plot. Often the joker's success depends on their timing in revealing the story's punch-line. Sometimes the joke works for the audience. Sometimes it doesn't. Comedians expect a percentage of jokes to fall flat and they bring with them such a repertoire of jokes that they can move from one to the next with ease. Sooner or later the audience starts to respond. Some professional speakers use the technique of delivering their rehearsed jokes or humorous lines from one spot in the room. Before long, if the strategy works, the audience begins to laugh as soon as the speaker moves in the direction of that spot.

To me, spontaneous humour is the real wit because it illustrates the power of intelligence, perception, observation and understanding. It is a response which grows out of the conversational flow. It is usually expressed in just a few words, obeying Shakespeare's dictum in *Hamlet* that 'brevity is the soul of wit'. It often involves re-framing the literal meaning of what is said. Take this exchange, attributed to pope John XXIII:

Question: **How many people work in the Vatican?**
Answer: **About half.**

In just two words, the pope had shown his wit and verve.

Storytelling

Stories and examples are vital tools in persuading every type of personality to your point of view. The words 'for example' are two very persuasive words, not in themselves, but for what comes after them. You prove your case through the power of your examples or stories.

Jesus and every other memorable philosopher and teacher spoke in examples or stories and parables. Jesus' stories were remembered for decades before they were written down by his disciples, Matthew, Mark, Luke and John. In cultures with an oral rather than a written tradition, the stories and lore have been handed down for millennia. They became the richest possession of the tribal elders whose solemn duty it was to pass them to future generations. The dreamtime stories of the Australian Aborigines are among the richest of such oral traditions.

Stories make abstract things concrete. Take, for example, the manager who tells his staff that 'everyone must work smarter'. The staff may nod reassuringly because they know it sounds right. But they can't really know what the manager specifically means. What makes the abstraction come alive is the example: 'For instance, George spends half his day getting formal approval for spending on office purchases. It is not a very productive use of his time.' So now they know. As Mark Twain remarked: 'Few things are harder to put up with than the annoyance of a good example.'

Television journalist and personality Ray Martin was once asked by the *Australian* newspaper who were the best people he had interviewed. He replied by naming Peter Ustinov, David Suzuki and a few others. 'They're anecdote machines,' he said. Being an anecdote machine is being a storyteller. It is explaining your points through examples. It helps people to understand and remember.

My friend John Bell was always turning over in his mind ways to say something more effectively or to enthuse other business leaders to take up social concerns. When he was asked to write a short biography of himself it became a wellspring of stories he could take with him whenever he spoke.

In working with John, I advised him to keep returning to this original source, to the stories which shaped him. It was inevitable that, when he connected these early stories to the issues on his current agenda, two things would happen. First, he would speak his own authentic story. It belonged to no one else. Second, like everyone else, he knew his own story so well that he had little trouble recalling it and speaking lucidly. His stutter, a trace of which was to remain with him for life, would mostly disappear when he connected to these stories. This was his *ethos* and *pathos* speaking.

Stories work persuasively when they have a point. A point gives a story focus. Without a point, a story just remains interesting at best or a diversion and annoying irrelevance at worst. Persuasive stories often have the structure of:

1 incident
2 point
3 benefit/pay-off

The incident is the story itself. The point may be expressed as: 'What I learned from this was . . .' The benefit or pay-off may be expressed as: 'What it means for us all is . . .'

Being Wholly Persuasive

You are not ready to be persuasive until you have prepared crisp stories, sharp examples and metaphors with which to illustrate what you are trying to say. For each point you wish to make, you need to ask yourself how you can make it clearer to the audience. As you prepare a business presentation, a media appearance or a negotiation, work hard to think of just the right combination of imagery, metaphors and examples.

Talking expressively needs to become a habit of mind. It should not just be reserved for those occasions when you speak formally or try to speak persuasively. Make it a goal to express yourself more anecdotally and metaphorically in day-to-day conversation. By practising in this way, you will find it much easier to express yourself persuasively on stage.

Practise talking in a more sensory way too. Try describing what is around you in visual, auditory, kinesthetic, olfactory and gustatory language. Sit by water and describe out loud what you hear. Watch a sunset and put it into words. Put the nose of an Italian restaurant to speech. Do it often so it too becomes a habit of mind.

CHAPTER 4

HOW TO PERSUADE
DIFFERENT PERSONALITIES

1 Persuading all comers
2 Why knowing about personality styles is a must for persuasion
3 Communication style profiles
4 Capacity for playing opposites is powerful communication
5 How do you see yourself?
6 How do others see you?
7 People you need to influence
8 Conclusion

All the world's a stage,
and all the men and women merely players;
They have their exits and their entrances;
And one man in his time plays many parts;
His acts being seven ages.
William Shakespeare, *As You Like It*

Persuading All Comers

Tom Peters made his name as coauthor of *In Search of Excellence*, the world's largest selling business book. The book got him into the speaking business, but it certainly didn't guarantee his success on stage, where he is a master of persuasion.

Have you ever been to a Tom Peters seminar? Peters is paid $100 000 a day to speak. He argues, cajoles, gets passionate, gets into details and is full of examples to illustrate his points. At his recent seminars I cast my eyes around to check the responses of the audience. They were enthralled. Mostly higher level executives, they were paying $900 a seat. The fascinating thing is that the book of this seminar, titled unambiguously *The Tom Peters Seminar*, which even includes the overheads he uses, sells for less than $20. Why do executives pay an $880 premium above the book price to see him in person? Well, it's like paying to see a rock concert or a sporting event, rather than watching the same event on television. People are buying the *experience*.

Any 'live' presentation is a show, and Peters is a great showman. But the real secret to his success is that he is a first-class psychologist. He understands how much pizazz, how much substance, how many points he needs to make, how much detail and how much empathy he needs to create to sustain the attention of his diverse audience for a whole day. So what is his winning formula? How much pizazz, substance, detail and empathy are needed?

Tom Peters intuitively understands how to satisfy audiences. He knows that his audiences are made up of individuals—individuals with very different psychological needs and learning styles. Over a session lasting some hours, Tom's success depends on his ability to address and satisfy those individual needs. Some need to know where the day's agenda will lead, others don't. Some want a few points, others want enough points to feel they are getting their money's worth. Some need summaries of the main points, others don't. Some will be persuaded by particular examples, others won't. Some will be fascinated by detail, others will be bored by it.

To capture each individual, Peters is dynamic with his content, his body language and his voice, working them together like instruments in an orchestra. They are all serenading the different personality types found in any audience, not just those who share his own way of seeing things.

But there are so many personalities, and they must all be offered something! If we are going to persuade them, we're going to need to understand them. Fortunately, there has been any amount of research into personality types, and what those types respond to.

Sir Francis Galton, a cousin of Charles Darwin, has been credited as the first person to use statistics and correlations to measure personality differences between people. However, like the study of persuasion itself, thinking about personality types goes back to ancient Greece. Curiously, though not altogether inaccurately, the ancient Greeks were convinced that personality was linked to body fluids. *Khole* was the Greek word for bile. Black bile produced a black or bleak mood. Yellow bile produced anger. Mucous phlegm in the body was considered a cooling influence. Happy, optimistic people had plenty of blood flow.

Naturally, the Greeks understood that people did not fit boxes and they imagined personalities fitting on two sorts of behavioural continuum, from sanguine—optimistic, in modern-day terms—to melancholic (pessimistic) and from choleric (angry) to phlegmatic (calm). Every personality-testing device today, with the notable exceptions of the coin-operated ones in amusement arcades or the quizzes for sex appeal in magazines like *Cleo*, still hinge on behaviour continuums where people are placed somewhere along a line between opposite types.

In our own century, Carl Gustav Jung's book, *Personality Types*, published in 1923, has had a defining influence on thinking about personalities. Jung, too, was fascinated by personality opposites and devoted his mind to analysing them. He invented the 'attitude' category of extrovert/introvert. Extroverts are outgoing and directed towards the outer world. Introverts are inwardly focused. Jung also adopted earlier ideas on certain 'functions'—for example, the split between thinking and feeling. Thinkers make decisions on the basis of logic and analysis. Feelers decide by values and individual worth. Other functional categories relate to how we experience the world. Intuitive types are driven by unconscious experience and perceptions. Sensate types are pretty down to earth and rely on concrete experience to form their judgments.

Ultimately, Jungian ideas underpinned the development of the personality-testing business and are central to the categories developed by the mother and daughter team Myers-Briggs. The Myers-Briggs Type Indicator divided the world into personality types along the three dimensions identified by Jung. They also added another dimension, judgers/perceivers. Judgers are people with a high need for closure and order. Perceivers are willing to go with the flow and see what happens.

Why Knowing About Personality Styles is a Must for Persuasion

Knowing about personality styles is essential for two reasons. It permits you to take a more objective look at yourself and gives you clues about how you come across to others. And it gives you vital information about how to persuade opposite personality types. Ultimately, it gives you the key to developing the content and style to maximise your potential to persuade everyone.

So, to have any hope of persuading someone else, you must understand their personality. But before getting to that base, you must understand your *own* personality. Some speakers get trapped in their own personality 'ghetto'. They present their arguments in a style and with the content which might persuade people just like themselves but which overlook what presses the hot buttons of others. If you can recognise the personality style within which you naturally fit, you can learn how to adapt your style to make a greater impression on your audience.

Naturally, the descriptions in this chapter are simplifications. There are any number of personality types. Individuals don't fit boxes. People frequently fit more than one of these types in some combination of personality traits. Different situations bring out different aspects of people's character. If you are unsure where you fit, a good question to ask yourself is: to which type would you retreat if you were in a stressful situation?

People who are flexible in adapting from one style to another have a decisive advantage in communicating with all the different types of people they need to persuade. Matching personality styles is akin to matching body language. Have you noticed how often you mirror the body language of the person you are talking to? This usually unconscious behaviour makes both parties in a conversation comfortable with each other. The same applies to personality styles. The people we talk to usually send us lots of signals about their personality. If we roughly match these signals with our own behaviour, it is an important part of building rapport. In other words, we get on to their wave length. If you get on to another person's wavelength, you are halfway to persuading them.

Communication Style Profiles

The industry of personality profiling, pioneered by Carl Jung, is a burgeoning one. Recruitment companies subject applicants to psychological testing for about half of all senior executive jobs in Australia. It will probably happen to you when you next change jobs if it hasn't already. The testing instruments used by head hunters measure people along all sorts of dimensions, with each company claiming the accuracy of their own approach—always very hard to test!

For the purposes of creating a manageable model for thinking about persuasion, I will confine my profile to just two of the dimensions identified by Jung, extrovert–introvert and thinking–feeling. This gives us a simple matrix of four personality types.

The Four Personality Types

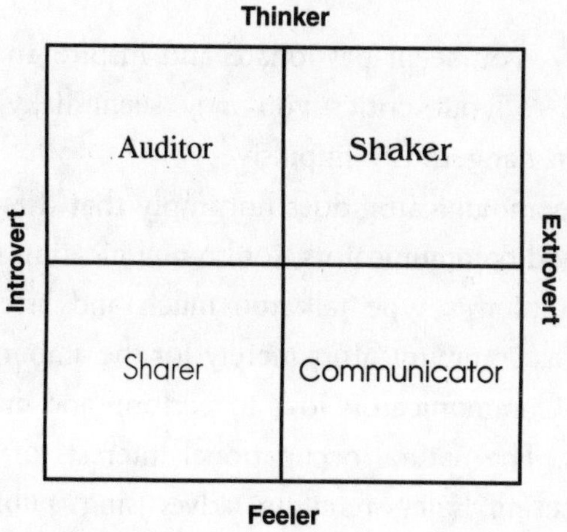
Thinker
Auditor
Shaker
Introvert
Extrovert
Sharer
Communicator
Feeler

The following two stories bring the personality types to life, and remind us how personality types do affect outcomes, more times than we'd care to admit!

Communicators

Communicators are extrovert feelers. If you are a communicator, you tend to be lively, carefree, intuitive, easy going, responsive, talkative, sociable and outgoing. You have the gift of the gab—

you're outgoing and happy to talk on subjects ranging from those you know a lot about to those you know only a little about. Caught red-handed at a robbery, you could talk your way out. You are passionate, energetic, enthusiastic, humorous, inspiring and possibly charismatic. You are a natural salesperson.

The problem is that some other people think you lack substance or sufficient depth in your knowledge to be persuaded by you. You come across to them as too glib. You do not seem to listen enough to others. You often seem to dominate conversations. Too often, you tend to think out loud before formulating your thoughts. People react cautiously to this and are not sure they trust you.

In summary, you seem passionate and inspire an enthusiastic following but to your critics you may seem flaky, egotistical, narcissist, even dangerously impulsive.

The term 'communicator' does not imply that these people are necessarily good communicators, for communication is a two-way process. Most of this type talk too much and listen too little. Many qualify as communicators merely for the amount of air time they occupy. Communicators love to perform and draw attention to themselves. The natural occupational interests of communicators are marketing, sales, retailing, advertising, public relations, politics, entertainment, training, journalism and broadcasting.

Examples of communicators include Richard Branson of the Virgin group who is quite happy to be photographed on a camel wearing Arab head-dress or in a bridal dress; Bill Gates of Microsoft (somewhat nerdy but a natural salesman); and Australian adventurer Dick Smith. It is the natural style of Tom Peters. Anita Roddick of The Body Shop shines with enthusiasm and flair and is a notable communicator. Some retailers who aggressively promote their own products on television fit this type too—Geoff Harvey of Harvey Norman, the Mintell man, and Crazy Eddy in the United States. Advertising leaders like John Singleton and fashion guru Simon Lock are notable communicators. So are many successful politicians such as Ronald Reagan, John F. Kennedy, Newt Gingrich, Gough Whitlam, Bob Hawke, Joh Bjelke-Petersen and Jeff Kennett.

Typifying the communicator type, Jeff Kennett once explained his impulsive style by saying: 'I'm not a committee person. Make a decision; get on with it.' The infectious enthusiasm of politician Barry Jones, broadcaster/writer Phillip Adams, and author Bryce Courtney make these primarily intellectually driven men also obvious communicators. The African-American evangelist tradition, spearheaded in the 1960s by Martin Luther King and in the 1990s by Lewis Farrahkan, is notably extrovert feeler in orientation.

How to Persuade a Communicator

Communicators respond to *pathos*. Communicators need to get excited about what they're hearing. They love stories and metaphors, anything to get some imagery flowing. They will respond more to your body language than to your argument. A logical argument requires concentration and detail—they'll be bored by the time you're finished! Make the point you want them to take on board, then reinforce it by using your inductive reasoning skills—plenty of colourful examples and pictured benefits of the action you're proposing. Keep up your enthusiasm.

If *they* like something, they're passionate about it, and will assume you to be as well. Allow them to get involved in your pitch to them—you won't be able to stop them! Bounce back their ideas as a catchy phrase or with a slash of humour—it will make them feel on board more than any delayed and considered agreement.

Whatever you do, make sure you are open with them. Communicators are ego-centred, which will often make them insensitive to your signals. Now is not the time for subtlety!

If You're a Communicator . . .

Play to your strengths. Spend time considering images and metaphors which will focus your message. In a business presentation made by a team, your natural role would be in making the opening or closing statements which require your flair for communicating passionately and with energy. Leave the detailed arguments to others. If you are presenting solo, make suure you work hard on the detail to persuade opposite personality types such as auditors. Be patient. Really listen to others. Don't get stuck in the communicator groove. Seek to win over shakers by being focused, auditors by reference to detail and sharers by building rapport.

Communicators

Character:	Extrovert, feeler, emotional, impulsive, talkers.
Need:	Excitement and sense of mission to be energised themselves.
Persuaded by:	Passion and enthusiasm for the big picture.
Body language:	Distracts.
Voice:	Many colours.
Dress:	Individualistic, considered, sometimes flamboyant.
Philosophy:	All the world's a stage—for them.

Shakers

Shakers are extrovert thinkers. If you are a shaker, you tend to be active, optimistic, impulsive, changeable, excitable, assertive, restless and touchy. You know what you want and how to express it. You are transparently ambitious for yourself, your business and maybe your country. You are decisive and forceful. You are good at getting your message across. Like communicators, you are an extrovert. However, while communicators are happy-go-lucky in their style, you are intense and focused. While communicators tend to make decisions emotionally, you are more rational. You come to the point and have a crash-through or crash approach to problems. You are persuaded by an argument which picks the main point in the case. You are willing to make tough decisions and stick by them. You are intellectually quick, and impatient with those people who can't keep up with your pace. That means you listen only selectively. You are egotistical but do not need to be loved or applauded in the same way as the more performer-oriented communicator types. You are prepared to throw your weight around to get things done.

The best of these qualities are enough to make you stand out as a natural leader. The problem is, some people think you lack compassion. They are not sure they trust you. You are sometimes too aloof and can get out of touch with the way average people think and feel. You are too cold and remote. In summary, you seem decisive but to your critics you may be arrogant. 'Shakers' are the self-styled 'masters of the universe'—for all the good and the bad that term implies.

In business, shakers are often at the top of the heap. They are not many in number but frequently hold down visible posts in the executive ranks of big business and some commercially oriented public enterprises. They are the generals and warlords. Merchant bankers, sports coaches, bouncers, the more aggressive lawyers and barristers often fit the mould. They are the entrepreneurial types in whatever occupation they choose.

Al 'Chainsaw' Dunlap is the archetypal shaker. He once managed the businesses of Kerry Packer, who himself is no wimp.

The Dunlap philosophy of life is that if you need a friend in business, you should get a dog. He has two dogs. Dunlap wrote *Mean Business: How I Save Bad Companies and Make Good Companies Great*. Tom Peters calls him 'one of the biggest jerks I have ever met in my life'.

The media have been dominated by the shaker press barons for decades. Rupert Murdoch is a shaker. You can see it in his work habits. His ability to hold together and manage such a large publishing empire is assisted by his habit of dealing with things on his desk only once. Canadian publisher Conrad Black also projects the shaker style. Ita Buttrose fits the mould. David Hill, former managing director of the ABC, is another. David Hill's mentor, Neville Wran, is a shaker too. He would demand that memos to him be written on no more than one page.

Former beer boss, aspirant prime minister and Carlton Football Club president John Elliott cultivates a tough man shaker image of himself. In politics, iron lady Margaret Thatcher is a prime example. Paul Keating's political style was shaker and so is that of Liberal politician Peter Costello. Lee Kuan Yew ran Singapore for decades in the sort of quasi-benevolent dictator style preferred by shakers. By now you know the type. If you cross a shaker, you will have a bloody battle on your hands.

The high-testosterone style of the shaker inevitably means that more men than women fit the category. However, Margaret Thatcher—known among some people as Tina for, 'There is no alternative'—is not alone as a notable exception to the rule. Hillary Rodham Clinton projects the comfort with power that goes with the territory. Another female shaker, the chancellor of the University of Sydney, Dame Leonie Kramer, once stirred the ranks of feminists when she stated that women 'wimp out' when the going gets tough. Shakers feel at home *only* when the going is tough.

There is usually a restless, hyperactive side to the way shakers behave. They fit what George Bernard Shaw described as the 'unreasonable man':

> The reasonable man adapts himself to the world. The unreasonable man persists in trying to adapt the world to himself. Therefore all progress depends on the unreasonable man.

How to Persuade a Shaker

Shakers respond to *logos*. You persuade a shaker by presenting a tightly argued case. What they want most of all from you is a focus on the main game or the bottom-line issue. Consequently, you need to be extremely well prepared. Brevity is critical. They will be impatient to turn their attention elsewhere. So get in, then get out.

If You're a Shaker . . .

Your greatest asset is to pick the real point in any argument. However, don't allow your natural impatience to get in the way of realising you must carry other people with you. Know when to go easy with your bulldozing approach. Don't get stuck in the shaker groove. Seek to win over auditors by reference to detail, sharers by building rapport and communicators by energy and passion.

Shakers

Character:	Extrovert, outcome oriented, quick witted, doers.
Need:	The point of the argument to be concise and transparent.

Persuaded by: One clear, reasoned, decisive message and plan
                     of action.
Body language: Blames.
Voice: Downward inflections at end of sentences;
                     sometimes harsh tone indicating forcefulness.
Dress: Powerful, classic and restrained.
Philosophy: Self-styled master of the universe.

Auditors

Auditors are introvert thinkers. If you are an auditor, you tend to
be moody, anxious, inflexible, rational, cynical, reserved, unso-
ciable and quiet. You usually know what you are talking about.
In fact, you are probably an expert in your field. You pride
yourself on your analytical and problem-solving skills. It's likely
that you have studied your subject area for years. You prefer to
think before you talk. You are rational rather than emotional in
your decision-making. You are persuaded by cool, logical and
complex argument. You are prepared, therefore, to listen long and
thoughtfully. You are steady and predictable. You disdain flourish
and flair as distractions. You are exacting. You demand order and
thoroughness in yourself and others.

The problem is, you know so much you are not really sure
where to start when relating your expertise to others. Or where
to finish. The detail of your subject often fascinates you more
than it does your audience, particularly if they are not your peers.
Too often you are so absorbed by your subject that you do not
notice people switching off. You don't seem to appreciate people's
limits for listening to such detail. In summary, you seem thorough
but you sometimes bore your critics.

In my work advising professionals on business presentations, I
meet far more auditors than any other type. They usually know

their subject area inside out but often find that expressing their knowledge in simple enough terms to be readily understood by their audience is painfully difficult.

Auditors are commonly found among experts in technical occupations requiring a great deal of detailed knowledge. Professional qualifications are the norm. Bankers, economists, lawyers, accountants, engineers and academics are typical auditors. So are pilots, architects and drafters, management consultants, administrators, computer programmers, actuaries and auditors. General practitioners and specialist doctors use auditor techniques in asking questions to check for symptoms. Where difficult choices are involved for the patient, they use careful auditor-type detail to describe the options and alternatives.

Auditor types are often the quiet achievers of business. It is a mark of their preferred operating style and retiring nature that their names are often unknown in wider public circles. A 1996 survey, reported by the *Wall Street Journal*, found that 70 per cent of chief executives are introverts. Their need for social interaction is 15 per cent lower than for the general population, with most of them relying on their own counsel. Says Richard Hagberg of Hagberg Consulting in California: 'People treat them more as a symbol than a human being . . . forceful, dominant, socially skilled. They can obviously turn it on when they need to.'

Former Reserve Bank governor Bernie Fraser is the archetypal auditor type. It is not just his carefully measured and cautious content but his flat delivery which marks him as a prime auditor. Other bank bosses typically fit the mould too—for instance, David Murray of the Commonwealth and Bob Joss of Westpac.

Judges often make an interesting variation on the auditor type. Retired High Court chief Sir Anthony Mason and another former High Court judge now Governor General, Sir William Deane, not only display their acutely analytical turn of mind when they talk, but it also shows in their clipped, precise manner of speaking.

The senior Canberra bureaucrat or mandarin is typically an auditor, by training if not by disposition. Nigel Hawthorn played the type perfectly as Sir Humphrey Appleby in the TV series *Yes Minister*. John Howard is a typical auditor. In this modern era of more 'managerial' state premiers, several (Jeff Kennett excepted) belong to the same list—Bob Carr and Richard Court of Western Australia, for instance. Nick Greiner, former premier of New South Wales, tended to treat public administration with the same analytical style suited to cracking a Harvard MBA case study.

How to Persuade an Auditor

Auditors respond to *logos*. They are persuaded by detail and analysis. They will want the i's dotted and the t's crossed as well as the basic facts. You need to supply auditors with supplementary papers and reports. Don't hurry auditors, because they will need time to digest your material. They do not respond well to pressure and deadlines. Be ready to answer the questions of auditors as they seek understanding and clarification.

If You're an Auditor . . .

In a team presentation, you should handle the detailed arguments, especially at the problem/solution stage. Allow others to fly with the bells and whistles. However, if you are presenting solo, think through and communicate with images and examples. Audit your voice and body language to see if you are lively enough. Don't get stuck in the auditor groove. Seek to win over communicators by showing energy and passion, shakers by being focused and sharers by building rapport.

Auditors

Character:	Introvert, thinker, detached, cautious, worriers.
Need:	Substance and detail.
Persuaded by:	Step-by-step logic, with both positives and negatives canvassed, supported by written documentation.
Body language:	Computes.
Voice:	Monochrome, monotonal; sometimes precise diction.
Dress:	Corporate-looking, clubbish, correct, subdued.
Philosophy:	God is in the detail.

Sharers

Sharers are introvert feelers. If you are a sharer, you tend to be calm, peaceful, reliable, controlled, even-tempered, thoughtful, careful and passive. You are a caring and nurturing person. You are deeply idealistic. People love, like and respect you. In turn, their affection and support are the wellspring of your energy. Like the good parental type that you are, you do not think about your own needs first. You have empathy for people and this influences how you listen to others, seeking the real meaning of what they have to say. This makes you a good listener. These qualities mean you stand out as a team player. Your sensitivity means you readily spot when other people feel left out. You like a consensus style of decision-making where everyone feels part of the action. You are slow to make decisions because you want to ensure that the feelings of everyone are fully taken into account. Intellectually, you are deeply uncomfortable with efficiency-driven philosophies such as economic rationalism because they put people second to profit.

You are an introvert, preferring and allowing others to

dominate the talking. Your emotional and nurturing sides dominate your rational side when you make decisions. If everyone felt
like you, the world would be a better place.

To your critics, there is a yawning gap between your idealistic
view of how the world should be and reality. People trust you
but sometimes doubt your effectiveness because your sensitivity
means you lack toughness. In summary, you seem caring but your
critics may regard you as not tough enough and therefore inef-
fective.

Occupational types that fit the mould are the caring professions
such as social and community workers, nurses, therapists, coun-
sellors, child care workers, and ministers of religion. Other
examples are school teachers, union officials and community
activists. In a better managed world, police would fit the category
but often they do not. Diplomats are sharers by training, if not
always by personal disposition.

Sharers are not widely represented at the top of big business.
Janet Holmes à Court is an exception but she achieved her job
in exceptional circumstances. Paul Simon, formerly of Wool-
worths, positions himself as a sharer. The Fletcher Jones company,
which pioneered employee ownership in Australia, became a
corporate sharer. James Strong, chief executive of Qantas, who
like a chameleon shifts from type to type as the situation requires,
is a sharer when he commits himself to talking to every person
inside his organisation to explain the company strategy and how
there is a role for every person within the big picture. Union
bosses like Jennie George and Bill Kelty are interesting examples
of people who can combine being both sharers and shakers.

Sharers can be attractive figures in politics. Bob Hawke was a
combination sharer/communicator. So was Ronald Reagan. Kim
Beazley, John Button, Bill Hayden, John Gorton, Tim Fischer,
Alexander Downer, John Fahey, Cheryl Kernot and Senator Bob

Brown are other examples of sharer politicians. Broadcasters Geraldine Doogue of Radio National's *Lifematters* and Caroline Jones, known for her long-running series, *The Search for Meaning*, are sharers.

On the world stage, Nelson Mandela is a notable sharer. Mahatma Gandhi was. Mother Teresa was the ultimate sharer type. So is the Tibetan leader in exile, the Dalai Lama, who is renowned for his warmth and humanity in responding to even the most difficult political questions.

How to Persuade a Sharer

Sharers respond to *ethos*. Build rapport with sharers. Relate to them so that they will relate to you. Be patient in building a relationship of trust. Be straight with them. Sharers, like auditors, do not respond well to pressure and deadlines.

If You're a Sharer . . .

Your ability to build rapport means that you are an excellent choice for first speaker in team presentations. If you are presenting solo, work hard on developing the factual case to persuade auditors and shakers. Do not be deterred if auditors and shakers do not respond with the same warmth with which you communicate because that is their style. Don't go overboard with gooiness. Work on examples and images to win over the communicators. Don't get stuck in the sharer groove. Seek to win over auditors by reference to detail, shakers by being focused and communicators by energy and passion.

Sharers
Character: Introvert, emotional, consensus-seeker, carers.
Need: Inclusion, recognition.

Persuaded by:	Connection and empathy shown by the speaker for the individual and social consequences of proposed actions. They want to see how the parts fit in with the big picture.
Body language:	Placates.
Voice:	Warm, upward inflections at end of sentences.
Dress:	Floral, paisley, practical.
Philosophy:	People do not care how much you know until they know how much you care.

Capacity for Playing Opposites is Powerful Communication

To some extent, the role we play depends on the stage upon which we find ourselves. Ronald Reagan illustrated this point when the former actor was asked by a journalist soon after being elected governor of California: 'Mr Reagan, what sort of governor are you going to be?' He replied, 'I don't know. I haven't played that role yet.'

As we mature, we play more roles in life. Shakespeare expressed it by writing of the seven ages of man. In our early years, we need to play only the role of a child. Young children learn about other roles through their play acting. As time progresses, we play the student, sports participant, lover, maybe soldier, husband/wife/partner, parent or carer. We make the transition from youthful worker with little responsibility to senior worker with numerous and complex responsibilities, then retiree. We often hear the expression that people grow into roles. This means, of course, that people learn the appropriate personality responses to the challenge of a new role.

Persuading someone else requires you to key in to the way

they like to process information. Don't talk just 'big picture' to an auditor, leaving out the detail. Don't just talk detail to a communicator, leaving out the 'big picture'. The following stories are examples of personality types in action.

Story 1

Helen is one of the nicest people you're likely to meet. Her closest female friends tell her that she is too nice for her own good. She lets some people, especially her teenage children, get away with blue murder. When pushed and pushed, even Helen sometimes gets to breaking point, feeling that people use her. Helen works as executive assistant in the busy office of a multinational company which markets a diverse range of consumer products like soap and detergent. She feels that she has a good working relationship with her boss, George. Certainly, George tells her that her work is outstanding and he wouldn't know what to do without her.

Helen hasn't had a pay rise in two and a half years. She and her husband, Bill, think it's time to confront her boss. Helen feels resentful about the fact that two of her workmates have received pay rises in the past few months but nothing has been said to her even hinting at the possibility. Bill is concerned about how tight the family budget has become since the extensions were added to create a separate bedroom for each of the boys.

It is three o'clock on a Thursday afternoon. George's office door is closed, which is not so unusual. He prefers to work quietly. Tentatively, Helen knocks. Before she gets a word in edgeways, George is telling her excitedly about plans for a product launch. When he finishes talking, he sends her a look which indicates that the conversation is over. George is very conscious about how he spends his time. Helen gets the message and leaves. That night when Bill asks Helen how she went asking for a rise, Helen skilfully changes the subject by raising Bill's favourite topic, what he wants for dinner. Deep down, Helen feels resentful about how people in her life manage to so freely manipulate her.

Helen is a 'sharer'. She lacks the assertive skills necessary to get her own way as much as more pushy people do. People like her boss, George, are 'shakers'. George is very task-focused and often forgets about the human goodwill which goes with the hard work necessary to notch up all the achievements of which he feels so proud. In a reflective moment, George thinks people like Helen are life's losers. Although they work as hard as anyone, they will never get ahead in quite the same way. George is prepared to bully to get things done. Helen would never go past pleading for cooperation.

Story 2

George is just back from an international sales conference held in San Francisco. These days he loathes long plane trips but there is something about the mists and moods of San Francisco which more than makes up for the tedium of the travel. The company knows how to put on a show. These international sales conferences are known for their good venues and their food, wine and entertainment. To most of the one thousand participants from all over the United States and the world, the formal part of proceedings, the speeches and reports, are the price that is grudgingly paid to enjoy the rest.

The company had recently appointed a new chief executive, Larry Fernes Jnr. No one knew much about Larry because his previous work had been outside the industry. On the first day of the conference, Larry was scheduled to speak after the morning coffee break.

Larry began by talking about values. His values. For a man, it went well below the surface to reveal what seemed like feminine vulnerability. He spoke about the illness suffered by his first wife and the impact it had on him in sorting out what was important in life. As George cast a glance around the audience of mostly men, he noticed that the majority were genuinely moved by what Larry was saying.

George, though, was getting a little impatient. He wanted Larry to get on with it. Where was he going to take the company? What was the bottom line? A few minutes later, George had his answers. Larry crisply segued to talking about the company's strategic objectives in the next one, three and five years. As Larry spoke in detail about each target, George found his mind spinning back and forth on the key messages, analysing them in his own way.

It was only later that he found out some of the detail from one of his fellow Australian managers, Sharon Schultz from Melbourne. Apparently Larry had spoken in enough particulars to really impress Sharon, who was renowned in the business for her nitty gritty attention to detail. Sharon is an 'auditor' type. She sometimes seems obsessed with detail to the point where she loses track of the big picture. But, if there was ever a flaw in the way a proposal had been put together, Sharon would smell it out.

As Larry signed off from the podium, he searched the eyes of the audience looking steadily back at him. He knew he had won. He knew it halfway through his speech. There was energy in the room. He let the energy take hold of him. In the last minute of his presentation, he gave way to the emotions he was feeling about the challenges which lay ahead to keep the company on top. As they clapped Larry off the stage, there was a feeling of excitement. For a moment, he felt he had captured some of the gospel-like buzz of those southern black preachers he had seen on television. He had always envied these natural 'communicator' types.

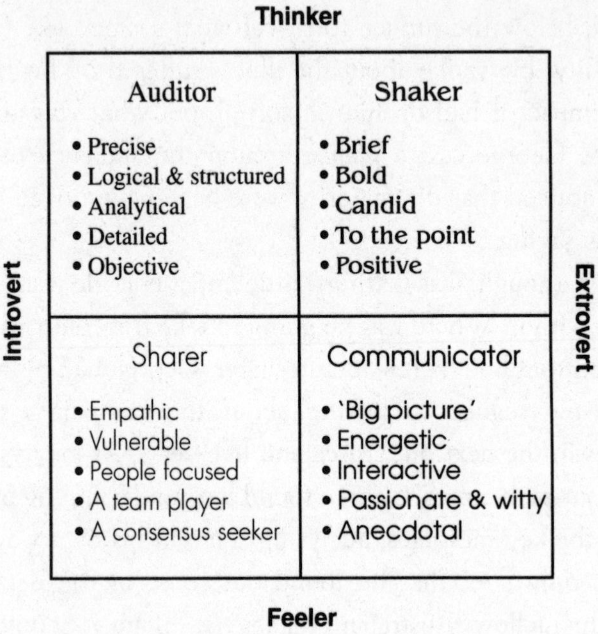
Thinker
Auditor
• Precise
• Logical & structured
• Analytical
• Detailed
• Objective
Shaker
• Brief
• Bold
• Candid
• To the point
• Positive
Sharer
• Empathic
• Vulnerable
• People focused
• A team player
• A consensus seeker
Communicator
• 'Big picture'
• Energetic
• Interactive
• Passionate & witty
• Anecdotal
Introvert
Extrovert
Feeler

Figure 4.1 Persuading different personality types

People liked what they heard. Larry had managed to impress even the cynics who know what these corporate rituals always produce. But Larry had got the mix right. There was enough empathy (sharer), enough substance (shaker), enough detail (auditor), enough excitement (communicator). Something for everyone.

Persuasive communicators are good psychologists. Whether they were conscious of it or not, the players in the two situations described above were acting out personality roles in a complex psychological game of persuasion. The object of their game was to get other people to freely say 'yes' to what they wanted.

Whether we are trading in products or services or ideas, persuasion is a lot like a sales transaction in which one person is

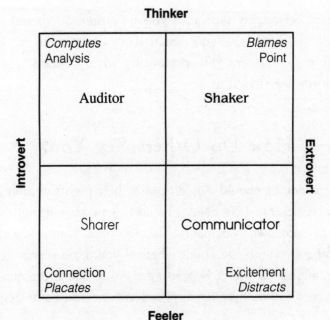

Figure 4.2 Communication style profiles

selling and another person is buying. The seller must always convince the buyer that they really need what's on offer.

As we know, people buy for different reasons. Some people buy emotionally and some buy rationally. Some people shop around extensively and others buy impulsively. The good salesperson copes with all types of buying psychology. The persuasive communicator copes with all sorts of psychological needs and behaviours in the audience they are trying to win over.

How Do You See Yourself?

Complete the communication style profile by shading the quadrants in Figure 4.2 which you think most represent your own dominant personality type(s). If you are unsure of where to place yourself, think of how you would react under pressure. Which type(s) most represent your personality when stressed?

I mostly see myself as a _____

How Do Others See You?

Just as a doctor should not diagnose their own symptoms or a lawyer represent themselves in court, you should not be the judge of your own personality. Get feedback from a few significant others in your life about whether you are a communicator, shaker, auditor or sharer by getting them to shade the quadrants in Figure 4.2. You may be surprised at how you come across to them.

How_____sees me.

People You Need to Influence

Think of two people you need to influence. Make sure that one of those you choose presents some difficulties for you in your relationship with them. Use the quadrants in Figure 4.2 to map where these people fit.

Person 1:_____
Their relationship to you_____
Person 2:_____
Their relationship to you_____

Do you find that the person who presents some difficulties in your relationship with them occupies a very different part of the communication style quadrant than you? Such an outcome is likely, although not necessarily certain. An ego clash over territory is common enough among people who are alike. What strategies might you employ to improve your relationship with the difficult person? Try writing down a specific plan for positively influencing the other person, including target dates for completing it. The plan may contain simple ideas such as calling by for a weekly chat on work projects or making an effort to attend more social occasions at which the other person will be present.

Conclusion

If you are a communicator, you excite others and can see the big picture. If you are a shaker, you get to the point and are decisive. If you are an auditor, you have substance and are strong on reasoning. If you are a sharer, you are the sort of person I would like to know because you care about others.

But, whatever you are, stop and think. Three out of four people are basically different personality types to you. To be persuasive, you must gain the confidence of the other types too. How are you going to press the buttons which will get other people to agree with you? Bear in mind that they will not be the same buttons as yours. Look again at the information contained about each type and what they need to know and feel before they 'buy' what you have to 'sell'.

A persuasive communicator is a person who has the flexibility to meet the other person on their own terms. If they are persuaded by detail, then you can anticipate their need and supply them with detail. If passion is what they need to be won over to your cause, then you give them passion. It was this very flexibility which made Larry Fernes Jnr's convention speech work for his audience. He addressed the needs of the different personality types who each wanted a message in terms to which they could relate.

Does this make the persuasive communicator anything more than a chameleon, that breed of African lizard known for their ability to change the colour of their skin to reflect their surroundings? Many politicians and other salespeople are famous for their ability to tell others want they want to hear. This reduces communication to a form of manipulation in which the message itself is changed in order to win the favour of whoever is listening. My own aspiration is to use the knowledge of personality types to help communicate the core of my message in a way in which others will understand on their own terms. To my mind, this is the ethical limit of the persuasive process. Being persuasive is not achieving agreement at all costs. The object is to create understanding and shared meaning between two people in the knowledge that the other person remains free to reject what I have to say. What does it mean to you?

CHAPTER 5

STEP-BY-STEP BUSINESS PRESENTATIONS

1 The Aristotelian secrets of persuasive business presentations

2 Step 1: Wearing your client's shoes—invention

3 Step 2: Time to think and organise—arrangement and *logos*

4 Step 3: Persuasive language—style and *pathos*

5 Step 4: Charts and speaker aids—delivery, *logos* and technology

6 Step 5: Non-verbal communication—delivery and *pathos*

7 Persuasive body language

8 Performance anxiety and warming up

9 Summary: Persuasive business presentations

CLARE JONES IS a brilliant young lawyer and communications graduate who works for Ambrose, a national consulting firm. The partnership, which has international connections, hired Clare to strengthen their arm at the increasingly competitive 'beauty parades' for winning new work. How business has changed. Gone are the days when firms would establish cosy client relationships which would last for a lifetime. Now the heads of consulting firms have to stand toe-to-toe against their opposition and persuade potential clients that they have the best credentials.

Beauty parades have become standard in many service industries. Advertising agencies have always been hired on the basis of making the right pitch to a selection committee of the client. Maybe half a dozen firms would be short-listed to pitch for the business. At separate meetings which would last for about an hour, the agencies would strut their stuff. There would be much talk about demographics and target audiences and positioning of the product and the sort of concept which would win the hearts and minds of consumers. It was a delicate balancing act because the agencies would not want to give away too much of their original thinking in case they lost the pitch.

Now beauty parades extend to other industries. Lawyers make pitches. Financial service groups make pitches. Consultants make pitches. In fact, Clare was hired because the partners at Ambrose were getting feedback that they were losing opportunities because their pitches were falling flat. Ambrose had done plenty of spade work to till the ground for winning new work, but they were falling down when presenting to the selection committees of potential clients.

At 10.30 on a Monday morning, Clare received a call from Fred Prosser, a senior partner in the firm. In two weeks, he said, Ambrose would need to pitch for work which would potentially involve one million dollars in fees. Clare's role was to organise the presentation and make it sing.

Clare immediately set about creating a time line on her office wall of everything that would need to be done. She was concerned about how little time was available. A preliminary meeting was set for noon on Monday involving the half-dozen consultants in the firm who might be involved in the project. The meeting was chaired by Fred but, trusting Clare's expertise, he deferred a lot to her.

After preliminary comments from Fred about the nature of the potential client and the project, Clare said the first priority must be to work out the purpose and message of the presentation. Some discussion followed about how the pitch fitted into the bigger sales effort. Fred remarked that, based on meetings he had already held with the client, he felt there was a 60 per cent chance of winning the job. He identified two people in particular who he felt would be critical in the client's ultimate decision.

Clare insisted that the discussion not move to other topics until a profile had been sketched of every likely member of the audience. Fred estimated that about six people would represent the client at the meeting. It seemed a little strange at first, but Clare asked Fred to tell the meeting about the non-professional interests of the people he had met. It emerged that one of the client's key decision-makers, George Smith, was a golfing fanatic. As it happened, the meeting was scheduled for the day after the US Masters would end. Clare kept a note of it, thinking it might make a good ice-breaker.

Clare said the next step was the most vital in the whole preparation. Deep thought needed to be given to defining the most critical questions in the client's mind. What did they want to know? What did they want to be assured of? What was important to them? 'If you were in their shoes,' Clare said to her colleagues, 'what questions would you want answered by the presentation?' It was funny, but when people devoted their minds to this, no one came up with the idea that the client wanted to know much about Ambrose. Fred offered the view that the client was probably far more absorbed by its own affairs and problems to care too much about Ambrose. Of course, Ambrose's capability was an issue, but it wasn't the dominant one.

After meeting for one hour, the group had agreed on a list of five questions which should be answered in the presentation. Clare was happy, but she warned that much more work lay ahead in identifying the key question. Clare said that every presentation should be organised around answering that one fundamental key question. Every other question would follow logically from it. As the meeting broke up, Fred nominated a committee of three headed by himself and Clare to take the work to the next stage. The third person on the committee was Joan Arthurson, highly respected as a finance whiz but with no direct connection to the project. Fred was keen to get an independent view of the presentation from the start.

When Clare got back to her office, she rang Gloria Mendez at the graphics support department and put them on standby to help with charts for the presentation. She asked them to attend the next meeting, scheduled for a few days' time. She also rang the potential client and asked for details about the planned room layout for the meeting. What technology was available? Was there a lectern? What sort of table was in the room? Would everyone be sitting around a table? Could a plan of the room layout be faxed to Ambrose?

By the time of the second meeting on Wednesday, Clare and Fred had roughed out a preliminary draft of the presentation based on the questions identified on Monday. Joan had made some comments and changes were added. Clare had convinced Fred that the best thinking and organising structure for the pitch was the four-part story, the one favoured by McKinsey and Co.

At the second meeting, Clare suggested that a major agenda item should be the selection of the presentation team. Fred was in. After all, he was the key client contact. Fred was good at making people comfortable. He also had the necessary *gravitas*. Clare thought Fred was the perfect 'sharer'. Alan was in. He was the chief number cruncher. He was a little dry, but he would bring substance to his part of the presentation and respond well to any unexpected questions on detail. Clare had her 'auditor'. The managing partner of the firm, Henry Barcoota, who had an established public image as the former chair of a high-profile government inquiry, would come along to briefly open and sum up the presentation. Everyone felt sure that his presence would signal how high a priority was being given to the project. That took care of the need for a 'shaker'.

There was plenty of argument about whether a fourth team member should be added. Clare was adamant. She reminded everyone that the client's selection committee had three men and three women. 'There must be a woman,' she said in her 'don't argue with me' voice. Opposition dissolved.

On Clare's advice, Julie McNamara was selected. Clare wanted to add a bit of pizazz to the show, 'communicator' style. Julie wasn't yet a partner of the firm, but would probably make it in the next few years. The case for Julie hinged on her track record as a presenter. She really had a way with words. She could talk in images. She sometimes even made bored audiences feel excited about an idea. Besides, Julie would be personally involved in the project. Fred thought it was a necessity to give the client a chance to assess the real people who would be doing the work, not just the heavies making the pitch.

Other things needed decisions. What charts? What technology for showing them? Clare thought the choice was simple. Computer-projected images were right for this client. They gave the high-tech feel. But a Clare trademark was how she convinced her colleagues to also use a flip chart. Going to a flip chart with a thick strong pen in hand gave the presentations a workshop-style spontaneity which clients seemed to like. There was one other thing: Fred always used charts as a crutch. Clare made her usual speech about the need to speak without charts 80 per cent of the time. Everyone in the room knew her standard line from memory:

'They have come to meet you, not your flippin' charts,' she would sigh. The following Monday, seven days before the deadline, was set for the next meeting.

The new week brought real progress. The draft of the presentation had been completed. Each of the four presenters had been responsible for drafting their part of the pitch. The whole thing had been hammered out on the word processor. Each presenter tentatively worked through their material. Gloria Mendez set up a multimedia projector so that the team could look at the charts. They were too wordy. Clare set Wednesday for the first rehearsal.

Come Wednesday, the presentation was beginning to look better. Content was one thing. But something had to be done about the presenters' lifeless body language and flat delivery. They looked as though they were attending a funeral. Even Julie was dull. Clare read the riot act. She set the final rehearsal for Friday. It would be a full dress rehearsal at which everyone would come in the same gear they would wear at the real presentation. Clare was a stickler on dress. She had once been impressed at reading a remark by Margaret Thatcher that, at important events, she would wear clothes in which she felt lucky. There was no corporate tie or any such uniform at Ambrose. But Clare had ordered the making of a simple lapel pin which everyone wore at formal events. It seemed to say 'team', but was subtle enough not to be embarrassing.

The whole show needed more work, but Clare was also concerned that the presentation should not be over-cooked. Being under-prepared is fatal, but there is also a danger in being over-rehearsed. Presentations need freshness to fire. It started to come together well on Friday. Monday was D-day.

The team arrived at the venue together. Their timing was just right. Enough time to be relaxed. Not too much time to get edgy. Fred was superb. In two minutes flat he had relaxed the audience and created some chemistry. Julie stole the show. The clients actually laughed. Alan got the tricky questions right. And Henry demonstrated why he was such a consummate politician, making the whole thing appear unified and committed. Ambrose won the work. At the debrief they drank the best champagne. Clare had one more idea. She contacted the new client to get feedback on why they had won.

Wouldn't it be great to have Clare on your team? She has a knowledgeable grasp of all the steps needed to prepare and deliver a great business presentation. This chapter is a step-by-step guide to preparing your next presentation, pulling together the same techniques employed by Clare.

The Aristotelian Secrets of Persuasive Business Presentations

The persuasive principles we use today in business presentations owe a great debt to the thinking of Aristotle's *On Rhetoric*. Remember that his rhetoric was divided into five principles or parts:

1 'Invention': identifying the key question
2 'Arrangement': structuring an argument
3 'Style': choosing persuasive language
4 'Memory': the Graeco-Roman habit of memorising speeches
5 'Delivery': the use of voice and body language.

Today the use of charts and speaker aids takes the place of memorisation. Otherwise, Aristotle's principles can be applied step by step to the preparation of a presentation, as can his principles of *ethos*, *logos* and *pathos*. The following pages show how.

Step 1: Wearing Your Client's Shoes—Invention

What Aristotle called 'invention', the identification of the central question which lies at the heart of the issue being addressed, remains the most important key to effective persuasion. I liken it to wearing your client's shoes.

Too many presentations look from the inside out, rather than the outside in. In other words, presenters remain standing in their own shoes. They prepare a presentation showing themselves off rather than looking from the client's, or outsider's, perspective and needs. Typically, they talk too much about the strengths of their own firm and how they are 'the best' in their industry. To the client's ears, the presentation may sound interesting, but it does not really get to the heart of their particular interests. The client's own agenda is what matters to them. After all, the client is there because they want you to do something to satisfy their needs. The client wants a solution to problems or an answer to questions. They probably don't expect an answer or solution right away, but their criteria for judging a presentation will usually be about the understanding shown for their needs.

The best way to get into your client's shoes is to ask yourself good questions. As Voltaire observed, 'judge a man by his questions, not by his answers'. Just as scientists search for the truth by asking themselves the right questions, effective presenters always start their preparation by asking themselves questions about the issue on which they are preparing to talk. Some questions will apply to every presentation. The real power of persuasion lies in identifying and addressing the underlying or key question in the minds of the audience. The right questions give the presentation focus.

Like Ambrose's Clare Jones, begin by writing a brief description of the topic of your business or professional presentation. The first question to ask yourself is: what is the purpose of the presentation? What are you trying to persuade your audience of? It is useful to think of some nouns and verbs which illustrate the purpose of your presentation. For example, nouns may include words like team, price, decision, future and relationship. Verbs might include words like choose, decide, create, win and negotiate.

Key Questions

- What are the key questions in the mind of your client?
- What is the question that your presentation is trying to answer?
- What are the three key arguments which support that answer?
- What are the specific benefits to the audience which flow from your answer?
- What action do you want your audience to take as a result of your presentation?
- Are there any message(s) you want your audience to hear which are not already covered in what you have written so far?

But Who Are You? Why Should Anyone Listen to You?—*Ethos*

'Know thyself' was the inscription on the Temple of Apollo at Delphi; Plato said it came from the seven wise men.

I have stressed the need to wear your client's shoes, but you also need to allow your audience to build confidence in who you are. You need to state your credentials without arrogance. This is what Aristotle called *ethos* or character. At the heart of your character are your values and beliefs. Your values and beliefs are told most authentically through relevant and concise personal stories.

Let me give you an example from my work in the media. Listening to people talk on radio and television has taught me that what really works as communication is speaking plainly from the heart. When someone talks abstractly about a topic—for example, 'I believe the government should . . .'—it may be interesting, but the audience has been given no compelling reason to listen. But when someone talks from the heart, such as about the loss of someone they love—say, from heroin—and then says what the government should do, the audience listens to every word with a completely different intensity and urgency. The speaker has given personal authenticity to their message through making themselves vulnerable by talking from their own personal experience.

Who are you? What are your values and beliefs? What qualifies you to speak on this subject? What special experience and understanding gives you 'standing' to authoritatively discuss this subject? How willing are you to share your own sometimes painful experiences to give authenticity to your text? All of these questions relate to the 'value-added' quality you bring to what you are saying. The issue is not who you are in general, but what you are in relation to what you need to say. So, to the list of critical questions above, you should add: What 'value added' do you bring to what you are saying?

Going to the trouble of writing down your organisational and personal values will make it much easier to express them. Your values are a set of specific guiding principles. If they are to have any real meaning, they need to be priorities for what you do, particularly in difficult circumstances.

A statement of your values will have more meaning for your client if it is supported by evidence or examples. You may, for instance, say that one of your key values is 'on time' delivery of your work. Of itself, this can sound like a woolly motherhood statement. It's the sort of thing everyone would say, isn't it? However, if you support this statement by giving an example of how your team worked around the clock to honour a particular recent contract, you have given real substance to your principle.

Don't be too afraid to make yourself vulnerable by sharing with your client. For example, disclosing what you have learned from past mistakes gives authenticity to what you are saying and brings to the relationship the candour and sincerity that will be missing in a slick sales pitch.

What really works in communication is being sincere, not being slick.

Can You Picture Your Audience?

To really get into your client's shoes, you need to think about to whom you are speaking. Your audience will be made up of people with different personality styles. An effective presentation will satisfy the needs of the whole audience, not just those who are like you. Imagine who would be in your hypothetical audience.

You may like to consider:

- their personality types: communicator, shaker, auditor, sharer;
- their age;
- gender distribution;
- their knowledge of your topic;
- their comfort with the English language;
- their seniority and power relationships with each other;
- their patience and willingness to listen;
- their need for detail;
- their need to be motivated;
- the extent to which they are already converted to your cause or argument or need persuasion.

Write a composite picture of one or two people in your audience. Remember that, in the Ambrose case study, Clare wanted a profile of each member of the audience. One key person in the client group, George Smith, was a golfing fanatic—not at all irrelevant when the presentation would be on the day following the US Masters. Here is a simple example of a composite picture of George, the golfer.

George Smith is 37 and a family man with three teenage kids. He is financial director of the client and has been with them for seven years. He is a member of the Hills Golf Club where he plays off a handicap of 10. He holds an MBA from Macquarie University. His wife, Anne, works as a part-time solicitor with a city firm. His body language is usually inquisitive but a little judging. He habitually sits stroking his chin. A conservative dresser, George definitely fits the *auditor* mould.

Recall Clare's concern about building a team that could reach every personality type in the client group. As the most senior member of the team, Henry, the managing partner, a *shaker*, would briefly open the presentation. Fred was a *sharer*. He connected well with his clients. He was the ideal choice to follow the opening. His mission was to build further rapport and establish a logical framework for the pitch. Julie, a *communicator*, and Alan, an *auditor*, had two tasks. Julie injected compelling example after example. She is an anecdote machine. Just as you can lead by example, you can persuade by example too. It was Julie's task to find just the right examples to fit the case. Clare knew that if the stories were appropriate, the audience would respond with nods of agreement. Alan provided substance and nitty gritty. The idea was to build a presentation in which there was something for everyone.

If you are presenting solo, you must learn the versatile art of satisfying the needs of all the personality types in your audience by yourself. The best presenters aren't stuck in their own style. They create their presentation to meet the expectations of each personality in the audience. This pathway to presentation intimacy is described in Chapter 4. You must meet each personality on its own terms.

Step 2: Time to Think and Organise—Arrangement and *Logos*

Aristotle said you've got to have *logos*, or reasoning, to be persuasive. At the Lyceum in Athens, the thinking and organising structure for a presentation was called the arrangement. The arrangement is like a coat hanger. Just as a hanger gives shape to your clothes, you need to give shape to your content. Presentations without a logical flow look like a mess of clothes lying crumpled on the floor.

The arrangements best suited to your presentation will of course depend on your situation—in particular, the personality types of your audience and the nature of the key questions that interest them.

If you need to convince your audience of your understanding of their problem, the four-part story may be the best structure. That way, your treatment of their 'situation' and 'complication' will convince them that you've placed yourself well and truly in their shoes. But if there's no doubt what the problem is, then a lively five-point plan would be the answer. Here you can concentrate on your proposed solution, showing it off in all its glory.

In either case, however, you will have to fit in a pinch of Aristotle's *ethos*—enough about yourself to convince your audience of your sincerity and abilities, but only enough!

Tell a brief story to which your audience can relate. Knowing that there are only 'six degrees of separation' between ourselves and anyone else on the planet, research your connections to your client's people and business and talk about it. If you relate to them, they will relate to you.

The five-point plan, four-part story and question and answer format, outlined in Chapter 2 are methods for arranging or structuring your way to a powerful presentation. Carefully choose the most appropriate format for your presentation after analysing the choices outlined in Chapter 2.

You should select the most suitable structure early in your preparation. It will save time. Once you have chosen your preferred format, take a page and divide it according to the organising plan. For example, if you choose the five-point plan, set out your page with the following headings, allowing space to make your planning notes:

1   Bait
2   Problem/question
3   Solution/answer
4   Pay-off
5   Call to action

Now, draw from your answers to the list of key points above to make a first draft of your presentation. Leave the bait blank for now as you can decide on it later.

Step 3: Persuasive Language—
Style and *Pathos*

Aristotle called the language used to persuade the audience 'style'. Once you have sorted out what you want to say, the next step is to choose the style with which to say it. Get the right side of your brain operating. What stories, images or metaphors will help glue your ideas into the memories of your audience? Your metaphor will give your presentation a focus. You need to choose metaphors carefully because they will stick in the minds of your audience long after you have finished speaking. How will they interpret them? Are you sure your image really sends the appropriate message? For example, if you are going to talk about the company's employees being as loyal as the Queen's corgis, you might get ready to be bitten on the ankle.

Clare was often told by the consultants at Ambrose that the sort of content they were dealing with didn't lend itself to metaphors. In reply, she was fond of quoting Albert Einstein, who said: 'Imagination is more important than knowledge.' Clare explained that they should try talking about competition in terms of a grand final, or leadership in terms of an orchestra working with a conductor, or teamwork in terms of the flow of a river. She stopped a meeting stone dead one day when she asked people to name an animal to represent their firm. Someone said a lion because it was sometimes hungry, sometimes lazy. Another person saw a donkey because it was too stubborn to adopt change. Clare announced that thinking about a subject in this way is what metaphor is all about. You are not ready to begin talking until you have developed ways of explaining your content in terms of something else. Chapter 3 suggests the almost limitless sources of metaphor.

In addition to choosing appropriate metaphors, you must think through what stories or anecdotes and examples will give lively support to your points. This is your proof for the points you make, enough for your audience to think that what you say must bear the truth. For example, if you say 'Our staff always work as a team', no one will be convinced. If you add an example of how your staff works as a team, you have given real meaning to what you say. 'Our staff always works as a team. After the recent fire on a Friday night, everyone in the organisation came to work on Saturday to help clear up the mess with brooms and mops. We were back working on Monday at 9 o'clock.' Now that is something. You need to develop such examples as proof for every point you make. The persuasion is in the stories. Note that your examples do not need to be long-winded stories. The anecdote about the fire took two sentences, or about ten seconds, to deliver.

It is your choice of illustrative stories that will give feeling to your subject, as well as contribute evidence for what you say. It is that feeling which Aristotle called *pathos* or passion, the third element of the art of persuasion. An audience is usually persuaded by a combination of logical argument and emotion. Stressing the merits of teamwork is logically desirable, but is an emotionally neutral concept. However, a team of people working together to repair the damage caused by a fire forge an emotional bond between themselves. Talking about this example to an audience gives the logic of teamwork an emotional dimension. It shows that people are passionate about teamwork. As a speaker, it would be hard to deliver this example without being passionate yourself.

Consider each of the three main contributors to *pathos* in our speech—metaphor, stories and humour—and decide how you can work them into your presentation. The more extroverted your audience (the greater the proportion of communicators and shakers), the more you will need them.

Step 4: Charts and Speaker Aids—Delivery, *Logos* and Technology

Aristotle's era long pre-dated the invention of the computer and the overhead projector, so you have a head start on him. Visual aids come into their own when you are condensing information. They are great at cutting detailed information down to a few phrases or images which can represent the detailed message without boring or overloading the audience. Charts can display an immense amount of information in a few seconds if sufficient thought is put into creating them. But without proper planning of their content and use, they can be a major distraction from your message.

The most important thing to remember is that visual support aids are there to support you, not supplant you. You are the speaker. Your audience has come to meet you, not your supporting aids.

Ask yourself the following questions whenever you prepare to give a presentation. Why has this meeting been called? Why have I been asked to speak? Invariably the answer to these questions is that people want to meet you. They want to have the chance to assess you, interact with you and ask questions of you. If they do not know you, they want to learn about your *ethos* or character. You will rob your audience of the chance to do these things if your presentation is dominated by your visual aids rather than by you.

The 80/20 Rule

The most boring presentation in the world is given by the speaker who stands up, and before even saying 'Good morning', turns on an overhead projector. The audience stares blankly at an overhead:

'ABC Corporation presentation to XYZ'. The talk is then dominated by a ceaseless stream of visual aids. These speakers ignore the principle that when it comes to supporting aids, less is more.

Visual aids are intrusive. When you switch on a slide or overhead projector, or boot up the latest software, you are asking your audience to look at them, not you. The light is powerful. The noise of slide and overhead projectors can sometimes make it uncomfortable to listen to you. In some venues the lights are dimmed and you, the speaker, disappear into the gloom. Your visual support becomes the real focus of attention because that is the signal you are sending. You are virtually saying to your audience: 'Look at them; don't worry about me.'

A small number of excellent visual aids will always have more impact than a large number. Having fewer aids draws more attention to them. Stick to an 80/20 rule. In most business presentations, the speaker should do without visual aids for 80 per cent of the time. Following the 80/20 rule means the speaker will dominate the presentation, rather than the visual aids.

One Chart, One Idea

There is a second measure you need to take to avoid splitting the focus of your audience. Avoid information overload on any single chart or overhead. Keep them simple! Gene Zelazny, in his book *Say it with Charts: The Executive's Guide to Successful Presentations in the 1990s*, says:

> a chart used in a business presentation must be at least twice as simple and four times as bold as one used in a report. It's the same as the distinction between a billboard that must be read and understood in the time you drive past it and a magazine advertisement that you can study in detail.

If the golden rule of using visual aids is not to use too many, then the silver rule is surely one chart, one idea. To keep your audience following your story, you must have them concentrate on one idea at a time. So, if they're looking at a chart, it must only show that one message.

Know Your Message

To avoid overloading your audience with information, you must be absolutely clear about your message. It is a common mistake for speakers to show people far more information than is necessary to support the point they are making. Introduce a chart by stating what conclusion can be drawn from it. That will guide the audience to interpret the data in the way you want.

Each chart should be headed by a message line. The chart should then have a label showing exactly what data it presents.

The message line of your chart plays the same role as a headline above a newspaper story. Compare 'January Sales Depressed' with 'Sales for January were depressed on the previous year's figures'. The first example is all you need. You, or the data in the chart, will explain that story.

Example

Message line: Stock X outperforms All Ords in every year by a magnitude of 3:1.

Chart label: Stock X versus All Ordinaries Index 1990–99

Once you are clear about your message, you can then choose the best chart to represent it. Your message will influence your choice of chart.

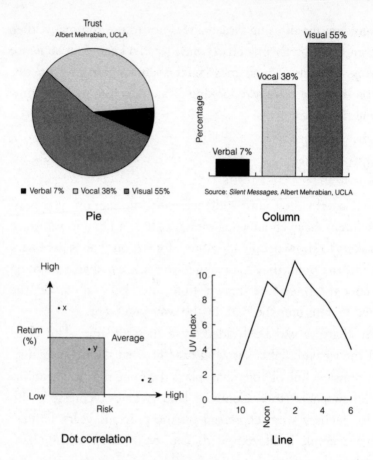

Figure 5.1 Four ways to display information

The Basic Charts

The basic charts for showing data visually are the pie chart, column or bar chart, line chart and dot chart. Each of these charts has a distinctive role in presentations.

Pie Charts

Pie charts are ideal for measuring proportions of a whole. People readily relate to these simple charts. They are not the way to go if you are comparing proportions between more than one thing. For example, two pie charts showing what proportion state and federal governments spend on education, health and the environment would confuse an audience. This comparison would be better illustrated by a bar chart.

In drawing pie charts, the largest proportion should start at midnight and head clockwise. If there are more than about five proportions, lump the smallest ones together using a term like 'other'.

Column or Bar Charts

A glance at a column or bar chart shows an instant ranking between things. The vertical axis shows what items are being ranked, the horizontal axis is a scale which illustrates the difference in magnitude and may be expressed as a whole number (e.g. sales figures) or some sort of percentage.

Choosing how to format your chart vertically or horizontally depends on which is easiest for your audience to read. The horizontal axis suits longer labels and time series comparisons.

Line Charts

Line charts are standard means of showing trends and distributions. They are superior to column charts for plotting time series data when the number of years being shown is large. For example, it looks far more effective to show the All Ordinaries Index performance since 1930 on a line chart than a column chart.

The line chart is suited to showing comparative trends. This variation is sometimes called a grouped line chart. It is also suited to showing distributions. It most commonly appears as a bell-shaped curve.

Dot Chart for Correlation

A common business need is to know comparative performance between two variables. For example, investors are interested in knowing the relationship between the risk of a portfolio and its return. We would all like to be in a low-risk portfolio with a high return. We all want to get out of a high-risk portfolio with a low return. These comparisons or correlations are best illustrated by a dot chart. Dot charts are commonly used by portfolio managers in their presentations to clients. They need careful explanation to an audience.

Other Diagrammatic Ways of Showing Relationships

While it makes sense to understand and use conventional methods of showing information, it's a good idea to look at books which have other interesting charts and learn from them. A few simple options are:

The Interconnecting System

The system chart shows how things are connected to each other. No one point is dominant. It fits with cybernetic and systems approaches to problems.

Scales of Justice

Where arguments are being balanced, the scales of justice can neatly summarise the main points for both cases.

Clock

The clock's obvious use is where there is a chronological order to what has happened in the past or will happen in the future.

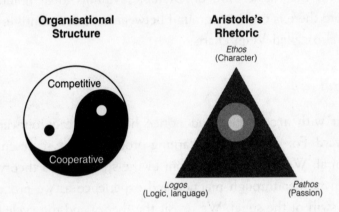

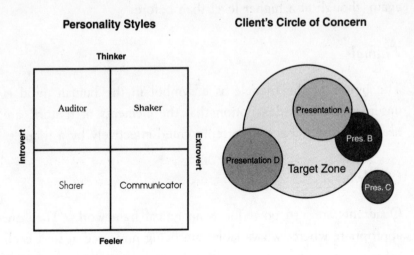

Figure 5.2 Give shape to your ideas

Concentric Circles

Concentric circles are suited for showing overlapping ideas. They are particularly effective where a core idea or value is surrounded by outer and connected ideas.

Intersecting Circles

This is the MasterCard or Olympic symbols look. It illustrates where there is common ground between separate identities. They are also called Venn charts.

Spiral

Start with a core idea and notice how it spreads outward and upward. For example, the learning process can be represented by a spiral. We start at the bottom of the spiral with a theory, then learn further through practice and experience as we proceed up the swirl of the spiral. We revisit the theory and the cycle begins again, though at a higher level than before.

Triangle

The power of the triangle as a symbol in the human mind is unsurpassed. Aristotle's notion that the elements of rhetoric are *ethos*, *logos* and *pathos* can be represented effectively by a triangle.

Quadrant

Quadrants are also powerful as analytical frameworks. They are appropriate where two variables are being measured against each other, as in the Boston Consulting Group's portfolio matrix: high and low market share being measured against high and low growth rate. This, of course, is an extension of the dot chart for correlation.

Star

Stars are suitable symbols where there are five parts to an argument or plan of action.

Cartoons

Australia has great satirical cartoonists. Using cartoons as a method of communicating ideas introduces humour into what might otherwise be dry content.

The Keep-It-Simple-Stupid Summary for Your Charts

Content

- Do not allow your presentation to be dominated by any aid. Keep to only a few lines of text on a screen or overhead transparency.
- Remove all detail you do not need to be read by your audience.
- Consider abbreviating sentences or phrases into a few words— for example, 'The message is clearer when it is summed up in only a few words', can become: 'Clear messages'.
- Each overhead should convey one idea only.
- Displaying spreadsheets has no place in business presentations unless discussing the spreadsheet itself is the point of the meeting.

Style Points

- Keep your aids looking consistent in typeface and colours.
- Use colour unless black and white is a deliberate style choice. Colours mean different things in different societies. Do not assume that your choice of colours is suitable if you are taking your materials abroad.
- Contrasting colours look visually most effective. Reversing colours out of your text can look sharp—for example, white text on a blue background.
- Add your corporate logo.
- Use icons and other drawn figures with caution; they have become clichés.
- Round out figures on your charts: 45.7 per cent should be 46 per cent; $171.2 million should be $171 million or maybe $170 million. You may need to say in passing that you have rounded out the figures.

Lies, Damned Lies and Statistics

- Be cautious if your presentation of data is too selective. You will affect your credibility.
- Avoid including only the data which support your argument.
- If your chart shows time series data, select the first year fairly rather than one which distorts the conclusion.
- Avoid using different scales on the same chart to artificially boost the appearance of one variable.

Choosing the Right Technology and Supporting Aids

When next you present, what support should you take? When and where are overhead projectors and computer-based presentations suitable? Is there a place for playing a video in your presentation? What are the merits of flip charts?

Choosing the right technology and supporting aids will help make your presentation a show.

The Case for Plugging in Your Laptop

Today there is no better speaker aid than your own laptop. A simple connector plug means that you can plug your laptop into a TV monitor or data projector. Staging companies have the technology to project on to large screens in conference venues and many conference and educational facilities now have the projection technology permanently installed. Boot up your graphics software like Powerpoint, Harvard Graphics, Presentations or scores of others and you are ready to go. Changing screens, audio and video clips is a cinch. Simply click.

That's the theory, anyway. The reality is not always so straightforward. At a national conference on technology and tourism which I chaired, many of the techno-boffins who were relying on their laptops as speaker aids found to their horror that their systems crashed just at the wrong moment. It became downright embarrassing, not to mention off-putting to their calm.

Laptop-driven speaker aids look high-tech and will give your presentation a professional and contemporary appearance. This will tempt you to over-use the technology and play second fiddle to it. Remember to stick by the 80/20 rule.

The Case for Multimedia

Your laptop is also the gateway to multimedia presentations in which you can mix moving and still images and sound, throw in a CD-Rom and download from the Internet to give your audience a total blast. But, unless you are a whiz at creating multimedia yourself, the cost of getting professional help in creating multi-media is high.

The down-side of multimedia is that it can overshadow the speaker. Keep to the 80/20 rule unless there are very good reasons not to.

The Case for Slides

There are strengths in using 35 mm slides, although they represent rather old-fashioned technology which is being used less frequently in business presentations. They provide excellent definition of the projected image and can reproduce photographs with superb clarity. Sometimes a combination of photographic image and text on the same slide can look extremely sharp and effective.

Slides are most suitable for venues where there are large numbers of people. The drawback with them is that they need a darkened room to be seen to best effect and that can be unsuitable in some situations. In the worst cases, speakers can disappear into darkness if there is no spot lighting provided.

Be wary of the potential for slide projectors to break down or jam at a crucial moment. This is particularly risky where the slide projector is used by many different operators. Many businesses and organisations do not conduct routine maintenance on their slide projectors, which are used until they break down.

The Case for Overhead Transparencies

Overhead projectors revolutionised business speaking and teaching aids. No lecture theatre would be complete without one. They are flexible technology, allowing the speaker to switch the order of transparencies at will. These standard-use business tools are most suitable where meetings have relatively few participants. Compared with slides, however, they project inferior image definition.

Overhead projectors are so easy to use that they sometimes tempt speakers into making little effort at preparation. I have lost count of the situations where speakers arrive at a meeting with a bundle of ill-sorted and ill-conceived overheads. The worst offenders are straight photocopies of other printed material. Photocopying documents or other written reports for use as speaker aids often mixes incompatible media. Effective overheads need to be stripped-down versions of material which is suitable for the printed page. Just as much thought and professional care should be directed towards preparing polished-looking overheads as for any other medium.

Colour transparencies usually beat black and white ones hands down in appearance.

Many overhead projectors are noisy and can be intrusive in business meetings and a distraction for people sitting near them. It is generally better to switch them off when you are not speaking to a transparency, but constant switching on and off can be annoying for the audience. Follow the 80/20 rule of speaking 80 per cent of the time and using speaker aids for only 20 per cent so there will not be a problem.

Using blank overhead transparencies with suitable marker pens will permit you to write up audience contributions.

Take along some methylated spirits to clean the glass of the overhead projector before you start. The dust and dirt on the glass will make your transparencies look grubby and ill-prepared. However, even after cleaning, you will find that scratches on the glass top of a projector will show through on your overhead.

The Case for Flip Charts

I work with at least two flip charts in nearly all my business presentations and training sessions because they allow me to work on twice the canvas. If I am breaking up the audience for group work, I ask for as many flip charts as there will be groups.

The case for flip charts is that they provide the most visible record of the work being done at the meeting. They can easily be displayed on a wall for the duration of the session or conference.

The limitation of flip charts is that they cannot be seen by large audiences. I would think twice before using flip charts in front of more than about 60 people. They should not be used where some members of the audience have to strain to see them.

I strongly urge you to buy your own very large pens for best effect. Change them when they start running low on ink and not when they dry out. Thick chalk can also look effective on flip charts, particularly to create a shading look. Do not rely on pens provided by the venue.

The Case for Video

Using video as a source for conveying ideas seems a natural extension of the everyday use of television and video at home. In my communication training, I use video as part of a multimedia mix to show excerpts from great speeches, examples of advertisements showing the five-point plan and illustrations of body language.

It is also invaluable as a teaching tool in recording and playing back people's performances. Evaluations of seminars consistently show that people learn more from watching their own performance than from anything else.

Give thought to how you can incorporate video into your communication needs.

The Case Against Whiteboards

Whiteboards are not a suitable aid for business presentations. Their place is at your own office meeting. They have a shiny surface which makes them difficult to read from any distance and whiteboard pens do not create enough contrast. Wheel them away.

The Case for 3D Models

Take something three-dimensional along to your next presentation. I have a kitbag of such speaker aids.

If I am talking about the right and left hemispheres of the brain, I display an anatomical model of the brain. If I am talking about different personality styles, I display examples of what necktie each type of person may wear (women do not have such an equivalent sartorial giveaway of their personality style). If I am talking about how we need to place our voice in the 'mask' of the face, there is no better way to make the point than to put on an actor's mask.

Your Own Equipment

Consider taking your own equipment such as slide and overhead projectors, software projection equipment, even TV sets and VHS monitors to important meetings.

When Presenting

- Keep to the 80/20 rule. Talk without support from aids 80 per cent of the time.
- Do not turn your back to the audience while gazing at a screen or obsessively look at your laptop.
- Do not allow yourself to be speaking in virtual darkness while your speaker aids are illuminated.
- Rehearse the use of your aids in real time to test whether you can explain them clearly and succinctly.

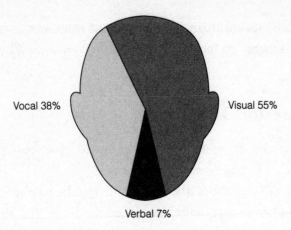

Vocal 38%

Visual 55%

Verbal 7%

Source: *Silent Messages*, Albert Mehrabian, UCLA

Figure 5.3 What we believe

- Rehearse with equipment to ensure it is working.
- Begin preparation of speaker aids with a long lead time. They take plenty of time to get right.

Step 5: Non-verbal Communication—Delivery and *Pathos*

In his lectures on rhetoric at the Lyceum, Aristotle taught effective delivery as a key dimension of the art of persuasion. It is not just what you say, but how you say it that counts. Delivery was about a speaker's non-verbal communication: voice and body language. No matter how good your content is, if the message contained in your voice and body language doesn't fit the words you are saying, no one will be convinced. If you don't feel committed to what you say, you can't expect others to. For example, the speaker who delivers the opening line 'I am really happy to be here today', but who looks like they would prefer to be anywhere else in the world is certainly not sending the message in their words. When there is a mis-match between the words and the body language and voice, the audience disregards the words and believes the non-verbal signals.

A famous study conducted by Albert Mehrabian at the University of California in Los Angeles, published in the book *Silent Messages*, found that where there is incongruity between verbal and non-verbal communication, the person receiving the message puts far more trust in the non-verbal content of the message.

Incongruity means that there is a mixed or conflicting message between the words that are being said and the tone of voice or the visual cues which are being sent at the same time. In the case of mixed messages, Mehrabian found that an audience puts only 7 per cent trust in the verbal content or words, 38 per cent trust in the vocal content or tone of voice and 55 per cent trust in the visual or what they see.

The power of body language is illustrated daily in the theatre of a court room. How many Australians jumped to conclusions about Lindy Chamberlain's guilt through reading the non-verbal signals of her behaviour? Chamberlain seemed disassociated. She was switched off. Millions wondered how a mother could fail to show more emotion about the devastating loss of a child. On the strength of this observation, many jumped to conclusions and judged her guilty.

In his fine novel, *Snow Falling on Cedars*, David Guterson writes:

In his face, he knew was his fate, as Nels Gudmundsson [defence lawyer] had asserted at the start of things: 'There are facts,' he said, 'and the jurors listen to them, but even more, they watch you. They watch to see what happens to your face, how it changes when witnesses speak. For them, at bottom, the answer is how you appear in the courtroom, what you look like, how you act.'

All of us know how to interpret the complex mosaic of non-verbal communication. We become skilled at reading the tone of voice and body language of our mothers from the earliest moments of life. However, although we don't need instruction about body language, we do need to be reminded about it. Some people ignore or don't read the signals coming from others. They wouldn't know if you kicked them under the table.

Persuasive Body Language

Many presenters are so focused on their content that they are unaware of the messages being sent by their body language. Being too focused on content and not focused enough on delivery is usually the mark of an under-rehearsed presentation. The speaker is spending all their mental effort sorting out *what* to say at the expense of *how* to say it.

A presentation is a performance. Stage fright or performance anxiety affects even seasoned pros. Laurence Olivier considered giving up the stage in his sixties because of bouts of uncontrollable nerves. As a presenter, you need to develop a positive and persuasive repertoire of gestures to show confidence in yourself and your message. You need to 'free' yourself to be yourself!

Your Eyes

- Maintain eye contact throughout the presentation. Wherever possible, seek out and make meaningful eye contact with everyone in the audience.

- Focus for at least a few seconds on each person so that you are meeting their gaze rather than looking through them or past them.
- Identify 'markers' in different parts of the audience to make sure you are reaching the whole room with your eye contact. Your markers should be friendly faces to which you return regularly.
- Don't read more than a few lines of a speech. It leaves you relating to the paper rather than to the audience.

Your Face

- Smile. This gesture will win more friends and warm up your presentation more than anything you say.
- Animate your facial muscles so that you can feel them move. Everything needs to be a bit bigger in performance than in everyday life.
- Avoid frowning even though the matter you are discussing is serious.

Your Hands and Arms

- Use your hands to paint pictures along with your words, to help get your words and meaning out. Hand movements will help animate your voice, face and body.
- Bold, sweeping gestures with your hands and arms expand your personal space and presence.
- Open your palms to signal trust.
- Avoid too many 'shaker' pushing down and 'sharer' plaintive gestures. The first can look too aggressive and the second too weak.
- Don't cross your hands in front of your crotch or behind your back.

Movement

- Move purposefully about the stage or even the audience. It helps energise the room.
- Consider mapping the movements you will make in the room as part of your preparation.
- Don't pace repetitively.
- Avoid getting stuck behind a lectern unless there is no alternative.

Practise

- Assess your performances. Get a trusted colleague to give you specific feedback about your body language.
- You will benefit from off-stage practice as you seek to improve the confidence of your on-stage body language. The bathroom mirror and videotaping yourself are good places to start.

Non-verbal Messages and Personality

In her book, *People Making*, Virginia Satir identified four behavioural modes, 'distract', 'blame', 'compute' and 'placate', which help us understand the delivery dynamics of each communication style:

- *Communicators 'distract'*. Their performance is their message. Their voice and gestures are colourful and robust. Desmond Tutu is an example of a communicator. Think of his lively face and exuberant, rhythmic voice. It excites. Can you?
- *Shakers 'blame'*. Their style is authoritative and sometimes bossy. Their sentences end with many downward inflections and their hand gestures push downwards as though patting a child on the head. Margaret Thatcher is an example of a shaker.

Is your persona assertive enough to use forceful body language when the occasion requires?

- *Auditors 'compute'.* Their style tends towards monotonal voice delivery and little or no gesturing. A variation of this, displayed by keen minds like judges, is a very precise and clipped delivery. Former Reserve Bank chief Bernie Fraser is an example of an auditor. Many people slip into auditor mode when they are very content-focused. It is fine for a time. However, do not get too stuck with a monotonous voice delivery and limited or no gesturing.

- *Sharers 'placate'.* Their style is meek and pleading. Their sentences end with many upward inflections and their hand gestures, often with open palms, lift upwards as though begging for agreement or common sense. Broadcaster Caroline Jones is an example of a sharer. Sharers connect. They win many hearts, but a sharer who is too stuck in the one groove may appear too timid. If you are a sharer, can you also shift to another style at stages of a presentation?

What non-verbal signals do you send when you are communicating? Your body language should match your message. For example, there is no point trying to connect with the audience in sharer mode if your body language is shaker. You won't sell your message well to an auditor if you are distracting like a communicator.

Versatile communicators are not stuck in any one style, but can access all of them during the course of a presentation. If you are making a team presentation, you can balance the different styles in your selection of who will speak.

Rehearsing

Clare Jones at Ambrose insisted on thorough rehearsal of the team presentation. She was right to do so. There is a world of difference between thinking about making a presentation and doing it. Every idea we have is a mental concept. Often we find it very difficult to know exactly what we mean in our heads, let alone express the idea in words. It is only when we express it out loud that we can test whether we really understand what we are saying. It is in the rehearsal stage that we get a reality check about whether we really know what we want to say.

Rehearsals also give a real-time check on whether we can make our presentation in the allocated time. Clock your rehearsal to see whether it fits the time allowed. Remember, it usually takes someone longer than they expect to say something—often as much as 50 per cent longer.

It is only when speakers are masters of their content that they can focus, during the presentation, on delivery and the body language cues coming from their audience. Under-rehearsed performers spend too much time inside their own heads working out what they are saying. Properly rehearsed presenters know their stuff and can focus on what the audience is telling them non-verbally.

Being a master of content doesn't mean being inflexibly locked into its delivery. Remember that excellent presenters know where they want to go but spend their time calibrating the audience response and reacting flexibly to it. Through reading the audience response or body language cues, it may be obvious to the presenter that something needs further explanation or repetition in order to be understood. A well-rehearsed, flexible speaker is most alive to responding to the dynamic needs of the audience during the presentation.

Although problems usually lie in presentations being under- rather than over-rehearsed, there can be too much rehearsal. An over-rehearsed presentation is dead and lacks spontaneity and responsiveness to the audience's needs. This is most likely to occur when the same presentation or a slight variation of it is delivered many times to different audiences. Professional performers overcome this hazard by thinking of the presentation as being brand new each time. To create something different every time, select a new story or example, change the bait, refer to something which happened today. Never let what you say bore you.

Performance Anxiety and Warming Up

Nerves affect every performer, but without them your performance would be too flat. However, there is a point where too much nervous anxiety starts to affect your performance adversely. So the trick is to find the happy medium.

Nerves work on your head and body and actions. Your mind races. You struggle to remember what you are going to say. Your body reacts. Your heart thumps. Your pores sweat. Your stomach has butterflies. Your mouth becomes dry. Your voice quavers. Your hands shake.

There is no complete cure for nerves, but there are several things you can do to make sure these miserable sensations don't overtake your presentation. What you must do is try several strategies and see what works for you.

The best insurance against too much anxiety is thorough preparation. Many people feel anxious because they are not adequately prepared and rehearsed to make an effective presentation. If you know your stuff, the confidence that knowledge gives you can overcome the worst of your presentation demons.

Visualising success works for some people. Spend time ahead of your presentation visualising yourself feeling confident in the performance. Imagine what it will be like to stand up ready to speak, hear the applause, then watch yourself make the presentation. This is the method used by sports psychologists to help people handle the pressure of big-time performance.

I go for the body relaxation trip. On the day of a performance, I try to find time for a swim or a good walk or even a massage. If you get your body to relax, the mind usually follows. If you know how to meditate, put aside a little time before an important presentation to help you relax your body and mind.

Another strategy which works before a performance is to take time to meet those people who will be in your audience. You will begin to warm to people and they will start to get to know you before your presentation. They will also be less inclined to 'judge' you on how you perform.

Consider integrating the audience into your presentation. Select someone friendly looking and ask them a question. Wait for their answer and use the information they have given you. Get ideas from the audience and write them up on a flip chart. This also has the benefit of creating an activity for yourself early in the presentation.

Breathing and Voice Exercises

Breathing is particularly important as your moment to speak approaches.

- Take some really long, deep breaths. Try to breathe in as far as your toes.
- Hold some of these breaths and count to five, ten, fifteen. As you exhale, visualise emptying out your tension.
- When you begin to speak, avoid long gasping breaths. Try short breaths to support short thoughts. John Wayne was once asked how he spoke a sentence of dialogue. He replied: 'First I say the first half of the sentence (pause) then I say the second

half of the sentence.' Even in a short sentence, Wayne had found space for an extra short breath.

- Warm up your voice. Trying to speak without a voice workout is like trying to run in a race without a body warm-up.
- Say the alphabet out loud, really stretching your mouth and tongue: a-a-a-a; aa-aa-aa-aa; aaa-aaa-aaa-a. b-b-b-b; bb-bb-bb-bb.
- Try some tongue-twisters:
  Red leather, yellow leather, yellow leather, red leather.
  Betty bounced a bright blue ball.
  Cuthbert lisps isthmus thus.
  Peter Piper picked a peck of pickled peppers. If Peter Piper picked a peck of pickled peppers, where is the peck of pickled peppers Peter Piper picked?
- Sing your favourite song or learn and recite an expressive poem.
- An unfailing technique to control nerves is slowing down. Talk *adagio*—literally 'at ease'. This is a particularly powerful technique if you have to read any part of your text and want to eliminate fluffs.

Experienced performers usually have less trouble dealing with nerves. Presenting over and over again gradually reduces nervous anxiety for most people, or at least makes them get used to it. However, your nerves will never go away completely. Nor do you want them to.

Using Notes

The convention in ancient Greece and Rome was to rote learn speeches. It is what Aristotle referred to as memory. These days, fortunately, we don't need to bother. Memorising gets too much in the way of spontaneity, but then few speakers can handle a written text. President Clinton is the only modern speaker I know who can make a written text come alive. He obviously rehearses it a number of times so that it is mostly in his head. As a result, when he delivers the text, he needs to refer to the written copy fairly infrequently. He also understands that a written text must be made to sound as though you are talking rather than reading.

Although I advise you strongly against reading a speech, there is still merit in writing the presentation out in full, particularly if you need to be precise in what you are saying. If you adopt this technique, you then have a choice. You can take the written speech with you and work from it during your presentation. If you adopt this choice, try to avoid the temptation to read out large parts of it. Your other alternative is to write out some shorthand notes of the longer written text.

If you have not written out your presentation, try to condense your notes to the minimum possible—in length, not size of words! I usually write prompts on an A4 page. For example, 'Franklin' would remind me to relate my experience in campaigning for Tasmania's Franklin River and what I learned from it. It is a mistake to have pages of prompt notes because you will spend too much time focused on them rather than relating to the audience. On the other hand, I also avoid small notes in the palm of my hand. It reminds me too much of the technique used in school debating.

Summary: Persuasive Business Presentations

To sum up, thorough preparation is the key to any successful presentation. Don't leave anything to chance.

Before the Day

- Identify key questions in the audience's mind.
- Create a profile of your audience. Include material that would stimulate all four personality styles.
- Decide on a structure to use—five-point plan, four-part story or question and answer format.
- Develop visual aids, keeping them simple.
- Write down the examples you want to use.
- Develop a metaphor for key points you want to make.
- Rehearse with colleagues.
- Rehearse in real time. How much time have you been allocated?
- Practise relaxation and voice warm-up exercises.
- Get to the venue early and become familiar with the room. For example, do you know where the light switch is on the overhead projector?
- Build flexibility into your presentations so that you can respond to audience signals.
- Pick out what you are going to wear well in advance. Ask yourself: 'Do I feel confident and powerful yet comfortable in the clothes I have chosen?'

During the Presentation

- Be aware of your nerves. Remind yourself that it is natural and expect to feel nervous.
- Be warm, be personal. Smile.
- Be positive. Remind yourself to lighten up.
- Use the point, reason, example structure in response to audience questions.
- Come alive—animate your face and voice. Be passionate.

- Communicate person to person—be personable, not declamatory, in tone.
- Be an anecdote machine—use parables, anecdotes and metaphors, and draw on personal experiences.

After the Presentation

- Ask yourself how the presentation went. What worked well? What didn't work? Draw lessons for future reference. Seek client feedback.
- Analyse whether you communicated your key messages.
- Go to see professional speakers make presentations and assess them. Learn to model the behaviour of effective presenters.

CHAPTER 6

THE ASTUTE NEGOTIATOR

1 What happens in a
   model negotiation?
2 Conflict and
   competition
3 Integrative versus
   distributive strategies
4 Successful negotiating
   is investing in a
   relationship
5 What happens when
   we negotiate?
6 Step 1: The five
   principles of
   negotiation
7 Step 2: Preparing
   for the negotiation
8 Step 3: How to
   apply your knowledge
   of negotiating styles
9 The framework for
   and stages of
   negotiation
10 The opening—
   building rapport
11 Tactics at the table—
   the middle stages
12 Closing a deal
13 Summary

What Happens in a Model Negotiation?

Successful negotiating in a business context is very demanding on
the participants. It draws on the widest array of communication
skills. Prior to the negotiation, a time and place need to be set.
Thorough preparation then begins, as each side considers the

context for the discussion and ponders their interests and positions. The astute negotiator also thinks comprehensively about the situation facing the other party. Homework builds a solid information base for establishing objective criteria for decisions. Where appropriate, careful team selection needs to be made, balancing personality styles and contributions. Brainstorming broadens the options being considered. Work is undertaken to weigh the consequences of what happens if the negotiation fails. Alternative solutions are canvassed and, where possible, firmed up (Aristotle's invention). Thought is given to the negotiating process, involving the preferred order in which issues will be dealt with and how differences will be resolved. Opening statements are drafted for presentation in point form (arrangement). Rehearsals reveal glitches (style and delivery).

As the parties sit down together, the theatre stage of the negotiation begins. Building rapport is the first priority. Managing the relationship between the parties and within each team remains a high priority, particularly if the going gets tough. Active listening picks up the nuances of the other party's statements and positions. Careful questioning helps unravel the interests which lie behind their positions. Objective criteria for reaching a win–win outcome are discussed. The common ground between the parties is identified and separated from differences. Tentative agreement is reached on areas where there is no dispute. Differences need to be tackled. A problem-solving approach is really what is needed now. How is the gap between the two sides bridged? Creative solutions are called for. Further questions reveal how both parties might move forward to resolve differences. The gap narrows as both sides make principled concessions. Final agreement is reached as the parties strive to achieve a satisfying outcome on both sides.

Once the negotiation is complete, the agreement is implemented and commitments honoured. A system of monitoring and reviewing performance alerts the parties to any problems.

Conflict and Competition

The model negotiation described above is based on the assumption that both sides cooperate to reach agreement. Negotiation ought to be a cooperative and not a competitive game. For this to happen, both parties need to approach the game the same way: you cannot have one-sided cooperation.

In reality, it is not so easy to be cooperative when both sides start with differences. Our society is organised around conflict and, unfortunately, much socialisation—especially for males—involves purely competitive game-playing. Many of our institutions, too, are modelled on the idea of conflict. Their intellectual origins owe a debt to the school of dialectics in ancient Greece. Dialectical argument is a three-step process. It involves putting a proposition, hearing the opposite point of view, and then forging a 'truth' somewhere in between. In Australia, our legal system, parliament and even the arbitration of wages are based on this model. The system entrenches conflict rather than collaboration to find the best outcome.

The problem is that many people play the negotiating game the same way. Their desperation to win or get their own way means imposing a defeat on the other side. Often they are not even conscious of their behaviour. They would be shocked to be told how the other party really views the result. 'Agreements' forged in this way aren't solid. The losers lose, feel disgruntled and seek to undermine the winner in some way. In business, relationships break down. In marriage, irreconcilable differences are the grounds for divorce. In politics, there's war.

Integrative Versus Distributive Strategies

Win–win negotiators bring an integrative or consensus-building approach to the table. They see negotiating as a cooperative and collaborative game aimed at resolving differences and strengthening the relationship between the two parties. They acknowledge the legitimacy of the other side's interests. They set out to accommodate those interests as well as their own and search for an agreement which expands the available pie and satisfies both sides.

Win–lose negotiators, however, are distributive or competitive in their approach. They see negotiating as a game in which the size of the pie is fixed, and the winner takes the biggest possible share at the expense of the loser. They do not acknowledge the legitimacy of the other side's interests and set out to gain as large a slice of the pie for themselves as possible at the expense of the other side. To them, negotiation is an exercise in dividing and ruling.

Conflict occurs—possibly irreconcilably—when at least one party adopts a distributive win–lose strategy. Rescuing the negotiation from stalling in these circumstances is not easy. Ideas for breaking such deadlocks are discussed later in the chapter.

Successful Negotiating is Investing in a Relationship

Let me share a plain truth. The people we deal with today are usually the same people we have to deal with tomorrow. And they are often the same people we have to negotiate with again at some time in the future. Indeed, in nearly all significant negotiations, the parties have an interest in continuing the relationship well past the time of striking an agreement. This may not be the case in buying a house or a car, but it is the norm in most business and personal negotiations. Goodwill is the bottom line of business. This reality places a premium on establishing trust. A trusting relationship cannot exist where one party exercises its power and dominance over the other. A negotiated outcome where both sides feel satisfied means a win–win outcome has been achieved.

What Happens When We Negotiate?

When two or more people sit down to negotiate, they have some things in common and some differences. What they have in common is that each side has something the other side wants. Their differences lie in the fact that both want the best deal for themselves. This might be the price of a car or a house. It might be someone's labour or talents. It might be conceding land for peace. The game of negotiating involves cutting a deal by settling the differences in a way which satisfies both sides.

The fact that alternatives to a negotiated outcome exist for both sides is what makes negotiation a test. Negotiation usually takes place in some type of marketplace. There are always other houses for sale. There are many different cars. In the job market, there is more than one person to do the work and always more than one job possible for the person seeking work. War is sometimes preferable to peace on lopsided terms. In this marketplace of alternatives, the effective negotiator should not be too intent on achieving a specific outcome. The buyer who has fallen in love with a particular house is in a weak negotiating position. Too much emotional investment in that one option greatly inhibits your ability to see alternative solutions. Your power is enhanced, on the other hand, if you are prepared to walk away. Naturally, your walk-away options are greatest when you feel there are strong alternatives to the negotiated agreement.

Step 1: The Five Principles of Negotiation

The principles of negotiation have their root in Aristotle's concepts of *logos, ethos,* and *pathos* which once again underpin the art of persuasion. Invention and arrangement—*logos*—inform each of the five.

1 Your information is the most persuasive tool you take to a negotiation.
2 The pie is never fixed and can always be divided in more than one way.
3 People are motivated by interests which lie behind their positions. Your questions are the key to unlocking the real interests of the other party.
4 Find objective criteria as the principle for agreement.
5 You need a walk-away alternative—a fall-back position—if things go wrong.

1 Information is the Most Persuasive Tool

Information in a negotiation is persuasive power. Every negotiation turns on information and most key information usually relates to considerations of time and money. If your information is weak, you may find yourself without a leg to stand on.

Much of the process of information-gathering involves learning about the other side's people and numbers. The information you need lies in the answers to simple questions. Who are the people you are dealing with? What sort of deals do they enter? What are the going rates in terms of time and money? Do they stick with their deals? What will it cost them not to enter an agreement with you?

Sometimes one side of a negotiation underestimates how much information the other side can put its hands on. In one commercial example, in a complex negotiation in Papua New Guinea over mining royalties worth hundreds of millions of dollars, the Papua New Guinea government had organised an on-line system which provided them with instant calculations on different payment scenarios. Their information system beat the mining company's system hands down, an advantage which was not expected by the mining company. Papua New Guinea was not going to be snowed on that agreement.

2 The Pie is Never Fixed

There is always more than one way of resolving a problem or area of difference. The more you build rapport with the other side and seek to understand their interests, the more likely you are to create solutions.

Sophisticated negotiators brainstorm on their own side and sometimes with the other side in order to devise a broad range of possible solutions. In international negotiations, there have been spectacular successes achieved by the brainstorming process, such as the secret Oslo meetings which led to a breakthrough in the Middle East deadlock. The meetings had no official status and were held among a small number of Israelis and Palestinians who had no authority to make a deal. This allowed participants on both sides to trade ideas without prejudice or commitment. Each side reported back to officials, who then cautiously adopted some of the proposals.

3 People are Motivated by Interests

As Roger Fisher and William Ury argue in their brilliant book, *Getting to Yes*, the core of effective negotiating is discovering the interests which lie behind the positions people take. Our interests are those needs which motivate our positions. If we understand the other party's interests, it is possible to begin exploring other positions which may satisfy their needs.

When the other party presents their positions on an issue, it is wise to search for the interests which lie behind them rather than accept them at face value or as non-negotiable. Put the position to the test of being explained. Ask: 'Why do you want that?' or 'What is your reason for saying that?'

Questions are the most powerful device a negotiator can use to get at the core of the issues that separate the parties. If you are prepared to listen and if you frame questions well, you will find out everything you need to know about collaboratively working towards a solution.

Questions are also the bridge to understanding the other party. In many instances, your questions will even help the other party get a better understanding of their own positions and interests. They are a check on the accuracy of your listening—ask: 'Am I right in saying that you believe . . . ?' or 'You have told me that . . .' They also help you test alternatives by asking: 'What if . . .?' As the negotiation proceeds, it will be time to check whether your ideas and problem-solving suggestions are acceptable to the other party. These questions always need to be framed with a reciprocal obligation. Ask: 'What would you do if I did . . .?'

Questions can help you save a negotiation which is in trouble.

Ask: 'Do you really want to reach agreement?' or 'What do you think would happen if our negotiation failed?'

Good questions helped unlock the difference between the interests and positions of Israel and Egypt over the disputed Sinai Desert. The Sinai is the strip of inhospitable land north and east of the Red Sea and Suez Canal which Israel occupied in the 1967 war. In the negotiations leading to the Camp David accord of 1979, both sides had fixed positions over Sinai. Egypt was adamant that Sinai must be returned as a condition of making peace with its enemy. Israel would not move because the Sinai had been the launch pad for a surprise attack on Israel.

In time, probing questions revealed the interests which lay behind Israel's position. The issue was not land, but security. Israel was not so much interested in a continuing occupation of Sinai as in guarantees of security and an assurance that history would not be repeated. A settlement was reached when Israel withdrew from Sinai but Egypt agreed that the desert would remain demilitarised to allay Israeli security concerns.

4 Find Objective Criteria as the Principle for Agreement

Finding objective criteria is the only way to persuade both sides that a fair and mutually satisfying deal has been struck, but what are objective criteria? The answer often lies in the way agreements have been made elsewhere. What does the market pay? What is the going rate? What are efficiency or professional standards or quality criteria? What precedents come from other judgments dealing with similar cases? How has it been decided in other negotiations?

Identifying objective criteria involves homework before the negotiation begins. Sometimes the information you need is on

the public record. At other times that information is a closely
guarded commercial secret which the other side will not divulge.
The difficulty is that both sides need to agree on what objective
criteria should dictate a solution. If you can strike agreement on
the principles of agreement, a solution will follow relatively easily.

It was once said that President Bush was such a bad negotiator
that he would pay full price for a Persian rug. I don't know a lot
about rugs, but I do know the principle of agreement has to be
the going rate.

Persian rug salesperson:	**This carpet is very cheap at $6500. I am losing money on it.**
Customer:	**The same one is down the road for half that price.**
Persian rug salesperson:	**No. That's an inferior product.**
Customer:	**It's all I can afford.**
Persian rug salesperson:	**It's a deal.**

Identifying objective standards helps remove personality issues
from the negotiation. A clash of egos typically leads the parties
to dig into their positions. Agreement about principles allows both
sides to move towards each other without feeling compromised
by the pressure to give in. Negotiation on objective criteria or
principles is the mark of the integrative approach.

5 Find a Walk-away Alternative if Things Go Wrong

Samuel Johnson noted that hanging concentrates the mind won-
derfully. A negotiation which is about to collapse has much the
same effect. To put it bluntly, you need a walk-away alternative
to give you leverage. Without an alternative, you are virtually a

prisoner to the terms set by the other party. This may be fine if the other party is committed to a mutually satisfying outcome. If not, you will be hung out to dry. This situation is dangerous for both parties because agreements reached in this way are likely to come unstuck.

Your walk-away alternative is really your bottom line. In many seminars I randomly ask participants what matters most in negotiation. Knowing your bottom line is the typical answer. To me this answer is both right and wrong. If by the 'bottom line' a negotiator means knowing their next best alternative, they are absolutely right to have a realistic idea of what happens if the negotiation fails. Too many negotiators only begin thinking about their walk-away alternative when the negotiation is on the brink. In these cases, they may have set their bottom line too high and it may be too late.

However, getting locked into a bottom line can make things inflexible. It actually negates what the negotiating process can produce. The negotiation itself should create the opportunity to think about the issue in new ways. Flexibility is a cardinal virtue of a negotiator.

Sports superstars—or at least their agents—are an interesting example of literally playing the walk-away alternative. Promoters want the superstars at virtually all costs. Golf tournament organisers are prepared to pay superstars like Tiger Woods and Greg Norman $300 000 or more as appearance money. It is only in recent decades, with the emergence of manager/negotiators such as Mark McCormack, that such sky-high incentives have been paid. Changes to the sporting/business environment made these negotiated outcomes possible. Television radically changed the economics of top-line sport through its capacity to deliver mass audiences which, of course, follow the superstars. Faced with only a 'no pay, no show' option, the promoters paid.

Step 2: Preparing for the Negotiation

Most of the deals that really count in your professional life are predictable episodes that can be planned months ahead. Yet, in many cases, preparation is left until the last minute, even though the parties must live with the consequences for years.

An approach that arrives at a thoroughly reasoned set of principles (*logos*) is what is needed. So, you should be intensive about your preparation when the time for the negotiation is approaching. Ask yourself the following ten key questions and write down the answers.

1 *What Do You Really Want to Achieve?*

What is your wish list? What are all your objectives in the negotiation? Don't aim too low. Don't aim too high. Don't go for an ambit claim.

What principles or objective criteria exist to make your claims realistic and your arguments persuasive?

2 *What Do You Want Above All Else?*

What are your two or three crucial objectives?

3 *How Can the Pie be Expanded?*

Looking at your answers to the first two questions, how can you expand the list of outcomes? How can the pie be made bigger and be cut differently? Brainstorm a list. Get outside advice.

4 *What If You Need to Walk Away?*

What is your walk-away alternative? Are you sure it is realistic? Do some homework on your walk-away options to firm them.

Wherever possible, do this work months before the negotiation begins.

5 What About the Other Side?

What do you know about the other side? What are their likely objectives? What is their likely position(s)? What interests lie behind their position(s)? What is your best assessment of the numbers which bear on their thinking? How could you package a win for the other side as well as your own?

6 What Is Your Own and Their Negotiating Style?

Who are you negotiating with? What personality style are they likely to bring to the table? How can you best influence them? See the section below on applying your knowledge of negotiating styles before answering this question.

Who can best represent your interests? Yourself? A lawyer or counsel? A team? Are your team's negotiating styles effectively balanced?

7 Where Does the Power Lie?

What is your best-informed opinion about who has the most power in the negotiation? What reasons support your opinion? If the balance is tilted against you, what information would help you change it in your direction? Does the other side have the authority to close the deal?

8 What Is Your Best Expected Outcome?

What *is* your best expected outcome? What is your worst expected outcome? What lies in the middle?

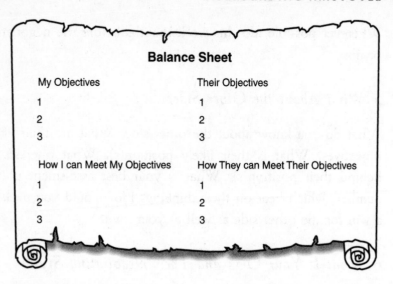

Figure 6.1 Balance sheet

9 *What Is Their Best Expected Outcome?*

What do you believe the other side thinks is its best, worst and middle outcomes?

10 *How, Where, When?*

What negotiating process do you propose? When should the negotiation begin? Where should it take place?

Write Up a Balance Sheet

After developing answers to the above ten questions, write up a preliminary balance sheet which includes the following considerations:

- your priority objectives and how the other party can meet them;
- their likely priority objectives and how you can meet theirs.

Step 3: How to Apply Your Knowledge of Negotiating Styles

Chapter 2 presented a detailed account of how to persuade different personality types, but how do you apply that knowledge to negotiating?

No one fits neatly into a box. Therefore, you need to be cautious about type-casting any person as one personality type or another based on a particular set of characteristics you observe. Your observations about their thinking and behaviour should be treated as clues to a complex personality type.

Communicators

Communicators are likely to be a hybrid mix, both distributive and integrative. They need to guard against being poor listeners and dominating the air time. This behaviour may obscure important clues about how they are really perceiving the negotiation. Ego-driven communicators risk imposing a win–lose outcome on the other side without being attuned to what is really happening. Being self-confident people, they are also likely to under-prepare. If they face another party who is well prepared, it may be difficult for them to recover from that disadvantage. Such a stressful situation may cause the communicator to be aggressive and dig into their position rather than work collaboratively with the other party.

Shakers

Shakers are highly competitive and focused on the bottom line outcome for themselves. This is the mark of a distributive negotiator who imposes a solution on what they perceive as the weaker party. Distributive bargainers create a win–lose outcome. Shakers are sometimes inclined to displays of bullying and temper tantrums to get their way. They are impatient and may be impulsive. Their self-assurance and short attention span mean they may under-prepare. They should avoid a crash-through or crash approach to negotiating.

Auditors

Auditors also are often a hybrid mix of integrative and distributive negotiators. Their patience and attention to detail are major assets in negotiation. Although not likely to be as submissive to aggressive behaviour as sharers, their own cautious natures may tempt others to try it on. They are likely to be better prepared than any other type. The risk is that their attention to detail may obscure the big picture. This could mean they are not bold enough in their aspirations.

Sharers

Sharers will be very integrative in their approach to the negotiation. They want both sides to be satisfied. They risk giving away too much. Their strong need for consensus can be self-defeating. This may create a lose–win outcome where the other side gains effortless concessions. They may not be sufficiently assertive in the face of aggressive behaviour by the other side. The sharer needs to guard against making unilateral concessions in which they give something away but get little or nothing in return.

The Framework for and Stages of Negotiation

Although there are a number of predictable stages in most negotiating situations, remarkably few negotiators start with a framework in mind about how the process should be conducted. Yet, as negotiation is as much about process as it is about substance, being first to suggest a framework is a distinct advantage. Naturally, a framework cannot be a rigid set of procedures and it will evolve as the negotiation unfolds. The sorts of matters which you should think about for the framework for your negotiation are:

- location and time—the where and when;
- discussion of the process itself;
- priority issues;
- discussion of principles;
- the order in which issues will be considered;
- issues which will be set aside for later consideration.

The framework should be settled between the parties in the opening stage of the negotiation. Almost every negotiation flows through three distinct stages. Knowing what to expect at each stage will give you a strong grip on the process, as well as the content of the negotiation. Without losing sight of your overall objectives, you can prepare for one stage at a time. The periods between the stages of the negotiation allow you the opportunity to think about and respond to what the other party is saying.

Opening Stage

This involves rapport-building, outlining the context for the negotiation, the suggested framework and process for negotiating, the principles or criteria which might apply to resolving the issues, initial proposals by both parties, and active listening by both sides to discover the interests which lie behind the positions adopted.

Middle Stages

The middle stage may take place over one or more meetings. Responses are made to the initial proposals of both parties. Agreement is sought over the order in which issues are considered. Further discussion occurs on positions and interests of the parties. Detailed discussion takes place over the principles or criteria which are to be adopted in resolving the differences that have arisen. Issues which are easiest should be dealt with first to ensure that momentum is gained. Difficult issues can be put aside for later discussions. Few major concessions will be made.

Concluding Stage

This is the agreement stage of the negotiation. A deadline is usually pressing and these pressures will force concessions to be made. Before proceeding, if you have not already done so, establish the principles or objective criteria which will dictate the terms of agreement. Our human tendency to procrastinate means that an 80/20 rule usually applies where 80 per cent of the concessions are likely to be made in the final 20 per cent of the time before a deadline. Do not make a one-sided concession without receiving something of value in return. Watch out for last-minute dirty tricks. Make sure every aspect of the agreement is recorded.

The Opening—Building Rapport

Negotiating is a theatre in which the negotiators are performers or actors. Like any performance, negotiating is often stressful on the participants. In fact, because important issues are at stake in negotiations, many people find the process among the most stressful of experiences. Thorough preparation is one of the best means of reducing this stress. Another productive way to reduce stress is to create an environment of rapport and ease with the other party. This process can begin well before the formal negotiating period.

Herb Cohen, author of *You Can Negotiate Anything*, compares national approaches to negotiation based on how much meaning is invested in people relationships on the one hand and the explicit terms of agreement on the other. Negotiators from nations such as Australia, Germany, Switzerland and Scandinavia put great store in the explicit language of negotiated agreements. At the other end of the spectrum, nationals from Japan, China, Taiwan, South Korea and Singapore put great store in the person with whom they are dealing. This concept helps explain the different cultural approaches to time horizons in which negotiations should take place. While the Australian negotiator is sometimes happy to cut a quick deal and run, an East Asian negotiator usually seeks a more protracted process at which social rituals play an important part in establishing formal rapport. Japanese and Chinese business people are reluctant to deal with others who aren't known to them or even part of their broader circle. Becoming an insider may never be attainable, but the outsider who expects to do business must be prepared to invest considerable time in developing a relationship of trust.

Listening and Not Being too Quick to Speak

Rapport-building involves a willingness to listen and absorb everything you can about the other party. Negotiation is a listening test. It requires patient, active listening to understand where the other side is coming from. You are likely to find out far more by allowing the other side to finish their points uninterrupted, even if their presentation seems to go on for too long.

The greatest block to active listening is your emotional reaction to what the other side says. As your emotions switch on, your listening is at risk of switching off. Active listening involves seeking to understand what the other side says without judging it. Another hazard which stands in the way of effective listening is mentally preparing to respond to the other side before they have finished. While your mind is occupied by your own thoughts, you cannot be absorbing what you are being told.

The normal conventions of back and forth conversation don't need to apply to negotiation. In day-to-day talk, we usually interact continuously in a flowing dialogue. In negotiation, it pays to be more hesitant and allow yourself time to think carefully before speaking. This gives you more time to listen fully and understand what is being said before you prepare your response.

Body Language

Body language—delivery, in Aristotelian terms—reveals the emotional state of participants in a negotiation. It can say far more than words do. Placing sole reliance on the verbal language of the negotiation is closing your mind to signals which can be far more important. People who are sensitive to the body language communication of the other side can detect changes in mood and atmosphere even before the other party becomes aware of the change. This is because some people are oblivious of the real signals that they are sending.

You should spend just as much effort auditing or monitoring your own body language as the signals coming from the other side. Nominate a member of your team to keep a check on the body language and vocal communication of both sides. If you are not part of a team, you must perform this task yourself.

Where to Sit

The choice of where to sit in a room in relation to the other party sends an important physical signal about the negotiation. Sitting across a desk or table from the other person is formal and tends to reinforce differences. If the boss sits behind their desk while they negotiate with you, they are telling you that they are still the boss and are not meeting you on equal terms. If they shift away from behind their desk and sit beside you, the relationship becomes more of a partnership. Whenever the height of a barrier separating people is lowered or removed—for example, by using a coffee table instead of a desk, the gap between the parties is reduced.

If you are seeking to create an integrative, problem-solving and cooperative atmosphere, the best option is to sit side by side. You are then literally working together side by side on the problem rather than facing each other across a divide.

The way we sit also sends an important signal. Negotiating sessions which last for hours are a challenge to the physiology. Unfortunately, very little furniture is designed for real body support. It is important to sit upright but at ease. Appearing stiff is a signal of discomfort. Sitting slouched is a sign of disinterest, boredom or low self-esteem.

Proximity to the other person is another body language signal. Proximics is the study of how people relate to each other in terms of space. Different cultures have their own rules about what is acceptable minimum space between people when doing business. Coming too close is intrusive and aggressive. Being too far away is isolating and remote. Country people usually need more personal space than city people.

The Eyes and Face

- *Maintain eye contact.* People look at each other more when listening than talking. It is typical for people to look at each other for about 30–60 per cent of the time they are talking.

It is often quite distressing for a person to be speaking when others are not looking at them. In the business gaze, strangers rarely look below the eye level of the other person. In a social context, friends extend their gaze to the mouth. Between intimates, the gaze extends to each other's bodies.

- *Look for signs of face tension in either party.* Giveaways are knitted brows and frowns, pursed and tense lips, locked or rigid jaw. It may be appropriate to lighten the atmosphere or take a break where there are obvious signs of such tension.

Hand to Face

- *Look for body language clues in hand-to-face gestures.* Stroking the chin or other parts of the face is usually a sign of evaluation. Another gesture signalling evaluation is cradling—placing the thumb under the chin and the index finger along the face. Watch out for whether the evaluation appears positive or negative.
- *Watch for other gestures too.* Pulling at the ear is a sign of doubt or a sign of wanting to speak. Head scratching is a sign of frustration or thinking, depending on the accompanying eye gaze. Hair twisting is often a sign of anxiety. Covering the mouth with the hand is what children often do when they lie. The gesture is to hide the untruth. The adult version of this behaviour is sometimes scratching the nose. But don't jump to conclusions. The person may just have an itchy nose.

The Body

- Open gestures make the person much more approachable.
- Arms folded, legs crossed and body closed in a protective position sends a negative signal about cooperation.
- Do not ask for agreement or a commitment when a person is

closed in their body language. They are likely to say 'no'. Wait for indications that the person is open and accommodating.

Voice

Listen for changes in tone of voice which give clues to mood swings. It may be appropriate to use the information in the form of a question—for example, 'You sound really tense when we discuss that matter. Why is that?'

Sometimes it's Better Not to Show Your Hand

Being open in your own body language will not always be to your advantage. There will be times when it is better to obscure how you really feel (if you can). Lawyers know this rule well. Peter Biscoe QC, a Sydney barrister, was quoted in the *Australian Magazine* as saying: 'If you see your case crumbling halfway through on no account do you change your expression.'

There will always be times in a negotiation when you do not want to reveal your feelings right away. You want time to consider a response rather than simply react. It is these times when you should be discreet about your non-verbal communication.

Tactics at the Table—the Middle Stages

In the heat of negotiations, tactics are sometimes employed which exert pressure on the other side. The best defence against these tactics being used against you is to know about them. The best counter-tactic is often to name them: 'Oh, you can't use that old trick with me.' Some of the key tactics are outlined below.

Middle stage tactics are:

- ambit claims;
- scarcity;
- aggressive behaviour;
- bad cop/good cop;
- equal time.

Concluding stage tactics are:

- making concessions;
- higher authority;
- the value of services declines;
- deadlines;
- last-minute claims.

Note: If you want to include positive tactics in the middle stage/concluding stage organisation, then:

- Middle stage tactics are:
  - Be doggedly optimistic.
  - Use metaphor to reframe negotiations.
  - Turn a deaf ear.
- Closing stage tactics are:
  - Resolve deadlock.
  - Think in terms of how the other side will sell the agreement.

Last-minute Claims

Negotiator 1:	So, it's a deal then?
Negotiator 2:	Yes. I think it's all sorted out. Just in time.
Negotiator 1:	Oh. There's just one last thing . . .

You may think agreement has been reached. As time runs out, putting you under maximum pressure, the other party introduces a significant new claim. The temptation is to give in to the claim rather than see the whole negotiation founder. A better response is to name the tactic and declare that if a new claim is to be entered by one side, then the whole agreement must be reconsidered step by step.

Higher Authority

Negotiator 1:	So, it's a deal then?
Negotiator 2:	Yes.
Negotiator 1:	Well, I'll just have to clear this with the boss.
Some time later:	
Negotiator 1:	The boss likes the deal but wants to make a few small changes.
Negotiator 2:	No.

This is a common enough tactic used in car and merchandise sales. During the final stages of the negotiation, it transpires that the person with whom you are dealing does not have final authority to close a deal. The other side has to clear the agreement with their boss. This means that your terms are set, but the other side can veto what has been agreed to by a junior negotiator. The aim is to force a one-sided concession. Don't budge.

Bad Cop/Good Cop

Bad cop:	You are not going to get a thing. You don't deserve it.
Victim:	That's not fair.
Some time later:	
Good cop:	He gets a little excited at times. Of course you deserve something. I think I can convince

| | him to make an agreement so long as you're not asking for too much or being unreasonable. |
| Victim: | **Oh, I am so grateful to you.** |

This bullying tactic is used in plenty of police stations (or at least in movies). The bad cop sets out to intimidate the victim. The bad cop is then called away and replaced by a good cop who, by comparison, appears to be the source of all reasonableness. The purpose of this tactic is to soften up the other party to make big concessions in the psychologically more comfortable presence of the good cop.

Aggressive Behaviour

| | **I wouldn't give you the time of day. You are completely untrustworthy. I find your performance totally unacceptable. Why should I bother to deal with you? There are people everywhere who want your job. And they could do it far better than you can.** |
| Bully: | |

Aggressive behaviour is psychologically one of the most difficult tactics to deal with. This game may involve shouting and even personal abuse. It is sometimes a blatant attempt to manipulate the atmosphere and destabilise or intimidate the other party. Khrushchev even tried it at the United Nations by banging his shoe on the table (it turned out that this was a third shoe, as he was still wearing a pair). It is often tried by parties who are under-prepared or feel they have a weak hand. It is certainly not the stamp of a person seeking a win–win outcome.

Do not react to aggressive behaviour. An aggressive counterreaction merely escalates the tension. You can afford to let an outburst pass. Do not attempt to negotiate in these circumstances. Point out that you are ready to negotiate when the other side is ready. Name the 'aggressive' behaviour and indicate that it is an impediment to the negotiation beginning.

Equal Time

Negotiator 1:	**Let me come to another key point.**
Negotiator 2:	**How can you justify what you've just said?**
Negotiator 1:	**I'd really appreciate it if you would allow me to outline my case first. Then I would be very happy to answer you.**

Another aggressive tactic is interruption. If you are interrupted, ask that you be given a 'fair go' and allowed to finish your remarks. Most people will back off when the other side pleads for reasonableness because they may not even imagine that their aggression is unreasonable. If necessary, you can stand up to signal that you wish to speak uninterrupted.

Ambit Claims

Negotiator 1:	**This house is one of a kind. The owner won't accept $1 less than $600 000.**
Negotiator 2:	**One of a kind all right. It's virtually unsaleable. It would be worth $150 000 at the most.**

Ambit claims are unrealistic claims, usually backed by rhetorical flourishes. Typical examples are a price set way too high or an offer made way too low. The party making the ambit claim hopes that the other side can be persuaded to split the difference between their price and yours. Don't be persuaded.

Scarcity

Signs: **Order now before it is too late! Last one! The offer expires today!**

How often have you heard these claims? They are the oldest sales tricks in the book. You need to be on the lookout not to be made a victim of this tactic in negotiation too. Robert Cialdini, in his book *Influence*, writes about how he made good money as a student by buying and reselling cars. His tactic was to arrange for potential buyers to turn up for an inspection at the same time in order to create a competitive atmosphere among them.

The Value of Services Declines . . .

Negotiator 1:   **I need the money now.**
Negotiator 2:   **What for? I'll pay you later.**
Negotiator 1:   **I need the money now.**

Members of the oldest profession know the rule that the value of services declines once they have been rendered. Thus they seek payment upfront. It is a dangerous thing to deliver the services while you are still negotiating their value, relying on the good faith of the other side to pay a fair price. You may not need the money first, but you sure need the agreement.

Making Concessions

Poor tactics:
Negotiator 1:   **We are only a few thousand apart. Let's split the difference.**
Negotiator 2:   **OK.**

Other poor tactics:

Negotiator 1:	I am prepared to concede . . .
Negotiator 2:	Good. Now we can agree.

Better tactics:

Negotiator 1:	What if I conceded . . . ? Would you give up . . . ?
Negotiator 2:	I would consider it.

An important principle in cooperative negotiating is that neither side readily adopts the approach of splitting differences between bid and offer. Rather, both parties need to search actively for principles which act as an objective benchmark for a satisfying agreement.

There will always be occasions, however, where it is time to make concessions in order to advance the negotiation towards agreement. It is foolish, in these circumstances, to make unilateral or one-sided concessions. As a general rule, if you are giving something up, you should insist on being given some concession in return.

Deadlines

Negotiator 1:	My plane leaves in two hours. You really have to bend in order to reach agreement.
Negotiator 2:	There are always other planes. The outcome of this negotiation will prove to be very worthwhile to you if you are prepared to be a little patient. We have to live with the outcome for years.

Time is always a factor in negotiations. As a rule, it is always scarce. The time factor is often used tactically when one side presses the urgent need to make far-reaching decisions. Artificial deadlines imposed by the other side need to be guarded against. You can simply refuse to accept artificial deadlines or create pressure of your own for the deadline to be changed.

The different approaches to time played a crucial role during the Paris peace talks on the Vietnam War. The American side was anxious to bring a quick end to the war. Their negotiating team rented Paris hotel rooms by the night. The North Vietnamese were in no such hurry to conclude peace. Their team bought a villa outside Paris.

Positive Tactics

While you need to be ready to respond when negative tactics are deployed by the other side, you should also be aware of a set of positive tactics which you can use to advance the negotiation and build agreement.

Be Doggedly Optimistic

Negotiator 1:   **This is getting nowhere.**

Negotiator 2:   **It's tough, but we must persevere no matter what. We are on the brink of an historic agreement.**

When the going is tough it is important not to become despondent about the outcome and signal that negative reaction to the other party. Do not create false optimism by being unrealistic about the actual progress of a floundering negotiation. If the negotiation is going off the rails, you are well advised to ask the other side a series of questions about their genuine interest in coming to agreement. For example, 'You do want an agreement, don't you?'

Use Metaphor to Reframe Negotiations

I know of many cases where introducing a metaphor to illustrate the state of the negotiations has helped reframe the situation for the parties. Sometimes a metaphor works in bringing one party to its senses.

Person 1:	**I will not be treated as a doormat and agree to accept whatever terms you offer.**
Person 2:	**I am certainly not treating you as a doormat.**

The metaphor you have in your head about the negotiating process itself is an important clue to your behaviour. You may not even be aware of this metaphor. It can be either implicit or explicit. Is negotiating a battle or chess game in which there are victors and vanquished? Or is negotiating one aspect of a relationship between business partners? In a formal business partnership, such as a law firm or accounting firm, partners bring different expertise and inputs into the joint pool and take a different share of the profits based on an agreed formula. Another metaphor of cooperative partnership is the relationship between allies. Partners in an alliance sometimes have profound differences from each other but agree to work towards the same goals of common interest.

Turning a Deaf Ear

Kruschchev:	[We will obliterate you.]
Kennedy:	[I didn't hear that.]

On some occasions it is prudent to ignore things that are said in the heat of conflict and negotiation. At a crucial point in the Cuban Missile Crisis of 1962, Kruschchev sent contradictory messages to Kennedy, one highly aggressive and the other more conciliatory. Which position was the real one for the Russians? After much puzzlement and deliberation, the Kennedy team decided to pretend that the aggressive note had never been sent. In this volatile situation wavering close to war, they responded only to the conciliatory gesture. This response seemed to work as nothing further was heard of the threats made in the aggressive note.

Think in Terms of How the Other Side Will Sell the Agreement

Negotiator 1:   **Did I do a great deal today!**
Negotiator 2:   **They agreed. It's terrific!**

When the other party leaves the negotiation they will need to send a message to their side that they have achieved a good outcome. As a good negotiator, you should always bear in mind what sort of deal you are handing to the other party. As William Ury says, you need to package a victory speech for the other side.

Deadlock

Deadlocks are most likely to occur when one side or the other is trying to impose a distributive outcome. Thus the challenge in breaking a deadlock is to change the game to collaborative problem-solving.

- Practising the virtue of patience is your first need in the case of a deadlock. Worthwhile deals are worth spending time on.
- A good dose of infectious optimism is never harmful when the going gets tough. All human beings are subject to mood swings and despondency can kill a good deal in the making. As a team member, take responsibility for spreading optimism to both sides.

Point out how much progress has been made already towards a joint solution, even though there is still some way to go.

- Negotiation is a creative endeavour. An impasse means it is time to look again at the assumptions you have made about the other party. Have you fully understood their position and the interests which lie behind it? Are your interests clear enough to the other side? Look again at the universe of possibilities for generating fresh solutions which can satisfy the interests of both sides.

- Brainstorm ideas to expand the pie. This may be done by yourself or with your own team. Why not suggest a joint brainstorming session with the other side? One possibility is for some members of both teams to brainstorm without commitment at a separate session.

- In team negotiations, consider changing the players, especially if personality conflicts appear to be a problem.

- Try to put more than one issue on the table. If the deadlock comes down to non-negotiability about only one thing, creating movement may be seen as a back-down by the 'loser'.

- Try to divide the problem into its component parts. For example, if the deadlock is about money, introduce the time issue: 'I am not able to pay you that sum now, but what if I paid you in 90 days? Would you agree to that solution?'

- Consider inviting in a third party to mediate the problem. The mediator's role is not to dictate a solution, but to suggest a way forward to agreement.

Closing a Deal

Negotiations do not need to be brought to a conclusion or closed by lengthy written agreements. One of Australia's most important business deals, the Esso BHP agreement to explore Bass Strait for oil, was sealed by a heads of agreement which was only a few pages in length. The parties agreed to put in half the costs and take out half the profits.

The merit of a short agreement is that it emphasises the need for the parties to remain flexible in the future in dealing with issues as they arise. The real basis of the relationship is trust.

The concession and real agreement stage is usually reached quite late in most negotiations. An 80/20 rule usually applies. Eighty per cent of the concessions are made in the last 20 per cent of the time available. The negotiator who will succeed in this hothouse climate is one who remains flexible and creatively engaged in the process of seeking agreement until the very end. The worst approach is to rigidly stick to a position.

Summary

Consider negotiation as joint problem-solving in which you and the other party work to achieve a mutually satisfying outcome. Picture yourself standing side by side addressing the problem with the other side rather than face to face in confrontation.

Before

Conduct superior homework. Research and number crunch. What do you want? Why do you want it? Put yourself in the other person's shoes. Consider their needs.

What problem-solving principles should apply? What is fair? Consider precedent, market rate, comparative value, costs, standards. Brainstorm ideas. Search for solutions of high value to you and little cost to the other side.

What if the negotiation fails? Develop your next best alternative. Role-play the negotiation.

During

Offer a plan on how the negotiation should proceed. Patiently seek to understand the other side's positions and needs. Don't reject positions; probe what lies behind them. Ask questions to clarify the other side's needs, solve problems, test options.

Be flexible. Don't lock yourself into fixed positions. The pie is never fixed. Generate options to expand the pie.

Seek agreement on the principles for settlement. Yield to principles, not pressure.

Concessions should be reciprocal. Package a victory for the other side too.

After

Debrief and draw lessons from your experience.

Put in place a system for monitoring how the agreement is working.

Engage in a formal review process.

CHAPTER 7

DEALING WITH THE MEDIA

1 Your audience
2 The media: How journalists work
3 Making your news *the* news
4 The quotable quote and the irresistible sound bite
5 Ambushes and the difficult questions
6 Persuasive body language on television
7 Dress and appearance
8 Summary: Dealing with the media to communicate your message

MEDIA ATTENTION FOCUSES regularly on organisations, their chief executives or perhaps those nominated to speak for them. Sometimes that attention is predictable; at other times it is totally unexpected. If you find yourself having to talk to a journalist about some aspect of your business, the experience can be bruising—unless you're prepared. That few minutes of glare in the media spotlight can make or break your career. If the pressure is intense and you handle the situation well, it may help make you. But it can sure help undo you.

A senior government official is giving a television interview out of doors on a hot day. He is under the misapprehension that the interview will last only five minutes. Twenty minutes into the recording, he is asked a question and his mind goes blank. He doesn't respond for fifteen seconds. It's an eternity in television time. A current affairs program plays the unedited sequence in prime time.

A national company has a food poisoning scare on its hands. It offers no comment to the media and instructs its public relations adviser to cool down the fraying tempers of the waiting journalists. At the end of a long day, as the news crews prepare to leave their doorstop positions, she bids them goodbye, saying: 'Have a good weekend'. Unknown to her, a camera is rolling. Those flippant words became the company's only 'official' comment on national television.

National Mutual is estimated to have lost about $160 million in revenue after *Four Corners* broadcast a detailed report on its disastrous financial standing. In fact, the outcome would have been even worse for the company had it not been for the skilled handling of the situation by the managing director, Geoff Tomlimson. Tomlimson had been extensively schooled before he faced an interview with the late Andrew Olle at the conclusion of the taped report on National Mutual. Every conceivable question that might be put to the MD was extensively rehearsed.

The media can also be deeply intrusive into private life. Sara Netenyahu, wife of the Israeli prime minister, stopped a television interview for 30 minutes after she was asked point blank whether she had tried to block the appointment of a female cabinet minister because of suspicions that she was involved in an extramarital affair with her husband. She repeatedly got out of her chair and shouted at the interviewer. The discussion continued only after assurances were given that the offending section of the interview would be deleted.

In Australia, businesswoman Janet Holmes à Court, of her
own volition, told *60 Minutes* that she was not involved in
an affair with former prime minister Paul Keating. In one
breath, she amplified the rumours a hundredfold.

These real stories illustrate the dangers of facing the media.
Not surprisingly, surveys of chief executives reveal that handling
the media is the greatest fear many of them face. Bosses who are
totally comfortable in their own company environment can feel
out of control in a media inquisition. After all, the media is not
their business: it is the business of journalists. Of course, it is
usually too late to start thinking about how to handle the media
when the spotlights are turned on you.

Gaining control is at the heart of successfully handling the
media. The inexperienced media performer holds none of
the control levers. They are left to respond as best they can to the
journalist's questions, with no strategy for avoiding questions they
do not want to answer. They may be unaware of the need to
develop and communicate an agenda. They do not know how to
introduce their own messages into an interview. They do not
know how to prepare a television or radio sound bite with impact.
They are not conscious of their voice and body language or what
dress to avoid on television.

This chapter will guide you in dealing with the media. It
explains how the media work, what they want and how to act
when you are in their spotlight. First, you'll need to understand
the audience you're talking to, and the media you're dealing with.

Your Audience

Many people talk to journalists without thinking about the audience to which they are communicating. Even if they do think

about who's reading or listening or watching, they don't think much about the *ways* people use the media.

It is a fact that people tend to scan newspapers rather than read them in detail. Australian Bureau of Statistics figures on time use on culture/leisure activities show that the average Australian spends sixteen minutes a day reading newspapers. They listen to radio for much longer periods—101 minutes a day. However, when people listen to radio, they are inevitably doing something else—for example, driving the car, taking a shower, buttering the toast.

Television gets most attention, with the average Australian spending 172 minutes a day watching. However, as with radio listening habits, people rarely pay full attention to what's going on. Nevertheless, in cultures like our own—the United States and the United Kingdom, for instance—about 80 per cent of people regard television as their principal source of information.

The Australian Broadcasting Authority published a monograph, *Living with Television*, in 1993. After surveying 1204 people about their television viewing habits, it came up with the following data:

Programs watched with full attention

News	34%
Current Affairs	21%
Documentaries	19%
Movies	18%
Serials	18%
Sport	13%
Comedy	10%
Infotainment*	6%
Don't watch anything/unsure	16%

* *Infotainment refers to lifestyle programs such as* Burke's Backyard, Getaway, Healthy, Wealthy and Wise. *Comedy refers to programs like* Seinfeld.

This information reveals a very different picture from the days when the whole family gathered around the radio or television to listen and watch attentively. It is clear that people no longer devote their full attention to what is going on. People watch and listen with a split focus—they are doing something else at the same time. This means that viewers and listeners take impressions rather than detailed observations from television and radio.

Another study in San Francisco, reported in the *Bulletin*, discovered that 51 per cent of television viewers had no recall of the stories in a news bulletin they had just finished watching. Among the 49 per cent of those who could remember something about the news, the average recall rate on stories was one item in nineteen.

My own interpretation of this information is that, on the whole, television and radio create and reinforce stereotypes. For example, for years we did not notice the daily reports of the war in Bosnia because there was very little real change. 'Still fighting' was the daily media status of the story. This was consonant, or consistent, with our perceptions and attitudes about how things were in that part of the world. We did not expect anything else. Then, one day, the parties came together in Daton, Ohio, to negotiate. That day, people would have noticed the news because the stereotype had been broken by genuine change and new information. In other words, it is only dissonance or inconsistency which forces us to notice and adjust our interpretation of the world.

One implication of dissonance theory, first developed by psychologist Leon Festinger in 1957, is that we are slow to shift our basic attitudes and beliefs. When we watch television, listen to radio or read newspapers, our perceptual filters tend to reinforce the views we already hold rather than break them and form new ones. This is why it usually takes totally iconoclastic behaviour to force people to re-evaluate their attitudes.

I was in Tel Aviv in November 1977 when the brave Egyptian president, Anwar Sadat, flew to Israel to embrace his enemies and begin the process which led to the Camp David accords and his ultimate assassination. In one stroke, Sadat's symbolic gesture forced Israelis and Egyptians to rethink their views of each other. The Israelis I spoke to were genuinely awestruck by Sadat's bold move.

So if you want your audience to change the way they see you, it may be necessary for you to act inconsistently with what they expect. Audiences carry many stereotypes in their heads. They expect politicians to be evasive and not address the question being asked. They expect vested interests to be selfish and gild the lily in putting their side of the story. They expect big business spokespeople to play down the harm being caused by greenhouse gases and give blanket assurances about safety and health issues in their industry. They expect the farm lobby to dismiss concerns about over-use of pesticides. On the other hand, they expect environmentalists to look alternative in their dress and appearance and be strident in their demands. In reality, most stereotypes are amply reinforced by the behaviour of spokespeople.

Occasionally, a few people break the mould. Following the High Court's Mabo decision, Rick Farley, as executive director of the National Farmers' Federation, publicly advocated a sympathetic line on Aboriginal land rights. Somehow Farley's flexibility, reinforced by the impression he made via the media, carried the day against the conservative elements of the farm lobby. As a result, Farley and the NFF achieved considerable leverage in the negotiations on the framing of the new law on land rights. Down the road, the mining lobby took a predictably hard-line approach of no sympathy and compromise on land rights. Their attitude effectively marginalised them from the process.

Tailoring Your Message

Sophisticated media players tailor their message according to what television channel or radio station they are addressing. Each of the major networks has a quite different audience profile. For instance, in Sydney and Melbourne, women dominate the Channel 7 News audience while men usually prefer 9 News.

News audience profile

Channel 7	Women
Channel 9	Men
Channel 10	Younger households, outer suburbs, women
ABC	AB demographic—that is, highest income and education
SBS	AB demographic—that is, highest income and education; its charter includes multicultural emphasis.

To use this knowledge to your advantage you need to develop different language for the separate audience groups who watch each network. For instance, if you are addressing a 9 Network journalist, it makes sense to talk about the impact of your news on men. On the 7 Network, focus on the impact on women and families.

Example: Closure of the Newcastle steelworks

Sound bite for 9:	Thousands of men will lose their jobs.
Sound bite for 7:	Thousands of families will be affected.
Sound bite for 10:	Thousands of lower income families are affected.
Sound bite for ABC:	The whole Australian economy will be affected.
Sound bite for SBS:	Migrant families, in particular, will be affected by this decision.

In radio, some stations and presenters attract a particular type of audience. For example, top-rating 2UE in Sydney boasts in its own *Station Profile* that the popularity of breakfast broadcaster Alan Jones 'is universal—male, female, blue collar, white collar, high and low socio-economic groups'. It goes on:

> Recently Alan conducted a couple of phone surveys in his program. The first was with regard to the Member for Oxley, Pauline Hanson's comments regarding immigration— Alan received a staggering 37 000 calls in three and a half hours with 98.4% agreeing to her comments. Prior to that, Alan received 33 000 calls with regard to Premier Bob Carr's decision regarding the downgrading of the Governor General [sic] position—92% were against the decision.

Information like this should give you a clue about how to handle the Alan Jones audience, which is fed and responds to strongly conservative opinions. There is little point in directly challenging or baiting a populist broadcaster like Jones. If you are to be effective in this environment, you must work with the grain, without compromising yourself or your views. At the very least, this knowledge should influence your choice of examples. What can you say, or how can you say something, that this audience might agree with?

Picture Your Audience

Before talking to an Alan Jones or anyone else in the media, it pays to picture the audience to which you are speaking. Take the time to write a brief word picture of the people who are listening or watching. Where do they live? What is their age? What are their occupations? What are their likely sympathies? What are they doing as they listen to the radio or watch television? How much attention are they paying to the program?

I have pictures in my head whenever I broadcast. On radio, I imagine that I am talking to someone who is driving the car to work. In effect, I am sitting in the seat next to them. I try to talk the same way I would if it were literally the case that I was there. Obviously they are not paying their full attention to the radio. They are thinking about the traffic and the day ahead, too. I imagine other people at home getting ready for their day. It is a busy time so they are paying only some attention to the radio as they move from room to room, getting the kids ready for school, having a shower or buttering the toast.

On television, I try to picture just one person as the audience. My mind focuses on a fine woman, Ena, who lives on a mixed farm on the Great Dividing Range in northern New South Wales. The busy life on the farm keeps her well occupied but she also takes an interest in what is happening far beyond. I just talk to her as if I were sitting across the kitchen table.

Picturing your audience like this helps you communicate in a way which makes people want to listen and watch. You are communicating one on one. It is also comforting for me to know that people are not listening, watching and judging like a mass audience. There may be many people listening and watching at the one time, but they are not in the one place. So, you are each person's companion. It's a relaxing and liberating notion, isn't it? It greatly adds to my sense of control.

The Media: How Journalists Work

If it is in your interests to cooperate with journalists, then you must understand how they work and attempt to fit in with what they want from you.

Some things are constants. Shocks make news. Conflict makes news. Drama makes news. Human interest stories make news. Identifiable personalities make news. Oddity makes news. Occasionally, even good news makes news. Many people get depressed by how much bad news there is in the media. They are right up to a point. However, the sorts of societies where the media is dominated by 'good' news usually are not big on freedom of expression. A government censor is behind the scenes somewhere.

Journalists work fast. They want to break news and cover news as it happens. Tomorrow is too late. I recall working for the *AM* program when a damaging story was circulating about a motor vehicle manufacturer. Our program called the manufacturer for comment but was told that their office did not open until 9.00 a.m. No further help was offered. Our program ran with the damaging story without any reply from the company involved. If something spectacular is happening, you should be ready to comment on air with minimum notice. If you know the issue and have authority to comment, go for it within minutes if necessary.

Most journalists cover many stories every day. In a typical Radio National breakfast program I will interview a dozen different people on perhaps as many different subjects. Like most journalists, I know a little about many subjects.

The average newsroom journalist covers at least a handful of stories each day. Some cover scores. So don't forget that *you* are the expert in your field, not the journalist. The journalist who rings you may know nothing about your industry or situation.

This 'ignorance' of journalists or the worldly inexperience of young journalists is a common topic of conversation among people who deal with news organisations regularly, but there is a danger in developing a cynical attitude to journalists. Sometimes,

annoyance with the journalist can come across on air. I was part
of a conversation with a leading national figure in public affairs
who featured prominently in the media. Someone present asked
him why he always appeared so angry on television. He replied:
'The journalists piss me off.' However, to someone at home
watching him on television, it appeared that the person was angry
with people in general, not the journalist.

What a journalist usually needs most from you is a good quote
or, if it is television or radio, a good sound bite. A quotable quote
is the heart of any story. A good quote is one that is lively and
interesting and says something.

If you are going to appear on radio and television for more
than a quick grab, a journalist or producer will assess you as
'talent'. Do you have a real point of view? Can you put it
forcefully? Do you have enough to say to sustain a longer
interview? Is your voice interesting to listen to? Are you energetic
or dull? Do you appear to be unduly nervous?

In nearly every situation, a journalist wants to help you tell
your story, but you need to know what your story is in order to
communicate it. A journalist really appreciates it when the people
they are dealing with know what makes a good story.

When things are hot, journalists want to talk to the real players
in the event, not a public relations person speaking on behalf of
the company. Public relations and issues management consultants
can play a vital role in briefing an organisation on how to handle
media inquiries on key issues but, when it comes to the crunch,
a public relations spokesperson lacks the credibility of an insider.
Savvy public relations firms are the first to know that and advise
their clients accordingly.

Most journalists do not want a lot of background material.
They don't have time to read it. They need material that is
succinct. If you are briefing a journalist, one or two pages is far

better than a dozen. Unless the journalist is working on the same story all day, more than half a dozen pages will not be read.

The Average Journalist

Most journalists are young (in their twenties and thirties). All except senior journalists are not particularly well paid. Most young journalists are tertiary educated. Nearly all journalists sympathise with the battler. However, if a journalist is assigned to a specialist round (industrial relations or finance or economics), they tend to absorb the dominant values of people who work professionally in that area. An outstanding example of this has been the acceptance by nearly all finance and economics journalists of the premises underlying the level playing field philosophy pursued in the 1980s and 1990s by Canberra politicians and bureaucrats. Basically, however, journalists are trained to be sceptical. Journalistic scepticism partly grows out of the fact that journalists are often lied to. Therefore they do not necessarily believe you are telling the whole truth. At the very least, the journalist will expect that you are putting a positive spin on what you say. If they are any good at what they do, they will wonder about the other side of the story. Journalists are especially sceptical, if not cynical, about big business and bureaucracies.

Many young journalists make role models of tough and aggressive senior journalists like Kerry O'Brien, Paul Lyneham, Quentin Dempster, Mike Munro and Richard Carleton. This gives the young journalist a lot of front without corresponding substance. Some journalists will be rude to you. However, most journalists, even the aggressive ones, are conscious of a code of fairness. If they forget it, remind them. The journalists I know regard it as their primary ethical responsibility to allow all sides of a story to be told.

How Television Journalists Work

Ray Martin, of *A Current Affair*, is on record as saying, 'Show me an intellectual television program and I'll show you a dead one'. He made this remark in the context of a discussion he once held with Rupert Murdoch, who told him that an intellectual news-paper is a dead one. I don't know whether Martin means that an intellectual program is the same thing as an intelligent one. At the ABC, at least, he would have a real fight on his hands by suggesting that there is no room for intelligent television. Intelli-gence, after all, is the power of the mind to know, understand and reason. But, sad to say, the Ray Martin view seems to reflect the dominant values that rule the most powerful medium ever invented.

Television news is pretty simplistic stuff. So is a lot of television current affairs. It's so simplistic that television gets out of its depth in handling complex information. And if God delivered the Ten Commandments to Moses today, tonight's TV news would simply say that Moses went up the mountain and came back with two tablets of stone. In fact, if Moses wasn't followed up Mount Sinai by a camera crew, the story would probably not get into the news at all. A news or current affairs producer will usually look at the pictures before writing a script for their story. It follows that if you can offer the television journalist good pictures to go with your story, you greatly increase the chance of getting your story covered.

Television appears fast when it is broadcast, but it is a relatively slow process to put together a news story. It takes a lot of time to set up television lights and shoot a television interview. City traffic is slow, and moving around locations and back to the studio takes time too. Editing for television consumes more time. A fair rule of thumb is that every minute of a story on a news bulletin or current affairs program takes one hour to edit. That means that a five-minute story on *The 7.30 Report* will take five hours to edit, or a 90-second story on the TV news 90 minutes.

These logistical constraints mean that television producers and journalists usually have a very developed view of what their story line will be and how you will fit into it before they begin work on shooting an interview with you. They will often approach the story with a 'schema' or formula in mind about what the interviewee will say. They may even make suggestions to you about the words to use or the angle to cover. This is one stop short of putting words into your mouth.

The length of a 'grab' or 'sound bite' on television is now about six seconds. This means that you will barely get a chance to say more than one or two sentences in the finished report. The journalist will often wind up an interview once they have a usable grab. To gain most control in this environment, you must thoroughly prepare and rehearse your key messages and how to say them. Advice on how to construct sound bites follows later in this chapter.

The 'six-second grab' convention means that TV stories have little subtlety. Television is the medium of 'goodies and baddies'. If you are considered a baddie, such as a company which is pitted against a battler, then getting your own point across in this environment can be challenging, to say the least. The trivialising nature of the six-second grab has forced the BBC to consider banning them in favour of more discursive question and answer sequences. The BBC is particularly concerned about how experienced media operators like politicians can manipulate news reporting with the quick grab. The system allows politicians to sidestep answering key questions which demand more than six-second answers.

Evolution of a Television News Story

The chief of staff assigns a reporter and crew to cover a story. The crew will shoot the pictures which make up the backdrop to the story. The reporter conducts preliminary conversations with the 'talent' to be interviewed. Short on-camera interviews are then conducted to get a sound bite. On returning to the studio, the story producer and reporter will look at the video and write a script around the pictures. The sound bed is then laid down with the journalist's voice-over. Interview sound bites of about six seconds are selected and edited in. Finally, the pictures are edited to match the words of the story.

How Radio Journalists Work

Radio is the fastest medium. Its strength is its instantaneous ability to report things as they happen. It only takes a telephone to be connected to anyone or any event in the world. It would not daunt a radio journalist to hear about an event one minute and have something on air the next.

This means that if you can respond quickly and coherently to stories as they happen, you may get plenty of opportunities for radio coverage.

In radio, sound bites used in news are longer than in television. You may get a whole fifteen seconds to explain yourself! You need to prepare your sound bite for radio as thoroughly as you would for television.

Although it is true to some extent of all journalists, the good radio journalist gets through by asking simple questions. An experienced journalist will put considerable time into thinking through questions for more important or longer interviews. It usually doesn't take long for an old hand to think up questions which will be difficult for the interviewee. You must be well prepared to deal with this reality and avoid repeating the mistake of a leading businessman who told a persistent reporter from the *AM* program, 'I am sick of answering your bloody questions'. Mind you, the answer did not appear to affect this man's wealth. He is one of Australia's richest men. He obviously could afford to take the cavalier approach.

Radio journalists may invite you to the studio for the interview. This can provoke an anxiety attack for some people, who feel much more comfortable talking on the telephone in the familiar environment of their own home or office. Usually, an invitation to the studio is an indication that the producer expects you to be good talent. It is wise to accept if you want a better quality on-air result. Studio microphones and atmospherics are superior to telephone conditions. You will probably be given more time to tell your story. You may even be offered a cup of coffee. Ask for a glass of water in case your mouth dries up.

Beware of 'infotainers' like Alan Jones or John Laws or Derryn Hinch or Howard Sattler. For them you are a mere pawn in the game. These personalities thrive on taking the moral high ground. You might be their victim. It is an unequal contest. The talkback hosts know that when they talk over you, a technical device known as the 'ducker' means that they will be heard and you will not. The host also decides when to end the conversation.

Evolution of a Radio News Story

The chief of staff will monitor the numerous sources of news and information and will assign a reporter to cover a particular story. Specialist reporters initiate this process themselves. The reporter will contact the relevant authorities to establish the basic facts, then interview the key player and follow up by seeking reaction interviews. These interviews may be conducted face to face or on the telephone. The journalist is seeking a sound bite of about fifteen seconds from the talent. The reporter will edit the interview themselves and the sub-editor will check their copy for accuracy and style. This process is simpler than television and so the radio reporter will be assigned to cover many more stories in a day.

How Newspaper Journalists Work

Each newspaper has its own production cycle of deadlines which vary enormously according to what part of the paper your story is to be run in. For weekly papers, the deadlines are often days ahead of publication. Even at daily newspapers, deadlines for special sections and weekend feature pages involve a long lead time. At the dailies, deadlines for the news pages are early or late evening. This means that if a newspaper journalist calls you at 10 o'clock in the morning, it is a fair bet that they are probably just fishing for a story. The serious stuff comes later. If they call you back around mid-afternoon, they may really be interested.

Newspaper journalists do not face the same time constraints as their radio and television counterparts. They may even speak to you for half an hour or longer. They may say they are talking to you for 'background' or 'off the record' (see caution below). You will say a lot in half an hour. In fact, one prominent Australian expert has told me of her frustration at what she regards as the laziness of some journalists in virtually asking that she write their story for them.

A lengthy chat with a journalist involves some dangers. I find that people who are quoted in newspapers regularly complain that they are quoted out of context or the journalist missed the real point. Often the interviewee contributes to this annoying situation by saying too much. If you have too many points to make you can't expect the journalist to report faithfully the one which most interests you. You are presenting the journalist with a smorgasbord of choice. To limit this problem, it may be in your interests to set a time limit on the discussion and stick to it. Let the journalist know that you have an appointment to make or a plane to catch.

A newspaper journalist needs a quotable quote from you just as much as a television or radio journalist.

The best newspaper journalists, like the legendary Michelle Grattan of the *Financial Review*, have a passion for accuracy. They will ring you back after they have written their story just to double-check their copy. Happily, such diligence is not confined to the quality newspapers. The populist magazine *Who Weekly*, part of the American *Time* empire, follows a similar procedure. Others don't. I find it is sometimes wise to play a little dumb and say something like: 'Would you mind calling me back with the quotes you are going to use because I may be able to sharpen them up for you. I'm often not very clear about what I'm trying to say first off.' I do this not to seek a veto over what is used but with the genuine hope that I can be helpful to the journalist and myself. And they often call back when asked.

Evolution of a Newspaper Story

The editor, chief of staff and other key journalists will gather at a news conference where the day's priorities are determined. Staff will be assigned to cover the chosen stories. Specialists will focus on their own rounds. The newspaper journalist works the telephone, talking to the relevant players and developing their story. Good journalists double-check their information and the accuracy of the quotes they choose to use. Naturally, the importance of

the story will determine the space and position given to it. Once
the story is filed, it will be checked by a sub-editor for accuracy
and style. The author does not write the headline above their
story.

Making Your News *The* News

Real news is telling the world something it doesn't already know.
Real news is a real scoop. Real news is scarce because it often
requires the work of investigative journalists to unearth. Richard
Nixon was brought down by the real news uncovered by
Washington Post journalists Bob Woodwood and Carl Bernstein
about the Watergate break-in and the Nixon-inspired cover-up
that followed. Real news sometimes comes in the form of a major
leak such as the boxloads of documents, known as the Pentagon
Papers, which detailed American involvement in the Vietnam
War. That leak changed the course of the war. Real news can
come in the form of an unexpected revelation in an interview. As
federal treasurer in 1986, Paul Keating said Australia was becoming a banana republic. It instantly changed the political and
financial landscape. That's when people will really sit up and take
notice. But remember that there is very little real news. In fact,
real news is so scarce that there would be no regular newspapers,
radio or television news broadcasts if editors waited until real news
occurred. So most news is manufactured.

Consider the remarkable array of happenings we call news:
political announcements (federal, state, local), parliament (federal
and state), council meetings, political parties, economics and
business, pressure group activities (consumer, conservation, femi-
nist, industry, chamber of commerce, farming, education, health,
welfare, RSL to name only some), opinion polls, court rounds,

police rounds (accidents and hold-ups, and so on), stock exchange and company announcements, sporting events and results, human-made disasters (fire, plane and train crashes, building collapses) and natural disasters (floods, bushfires, drought, earthquakes), royal commissions, public inquiries and hearings, medical breakthroughs and health, hardship and charities, lotteries, schools and higher education, agriculture, fashion, books, film, theatre, opera, dance and ballet, anniversaries, diplomacy and international relations, communications (television and radio programs), births, deaths and marriages, the royal family, personalities and gossip, film stars and models, astrology, science and technology, the public service.

To get your news in, you'll need more than just a fax and a prayer. What do you do if you want the news media to run your story?

A story needs a peg and so do you. Although there are literally thousands of stories we call news each day in the media, most do not occur in a vacuum. They rely on a 'peg'. A peg gives a story something to attach it to the news agenda. For example, stories on home heating depend on the peg of the onset of winter. It's hard to get a story up about home heating in the middle of summer. So if you want to get some positive news going about your home heating invention, wait until the onset of cold weather!

Example of Story and Peg

Story:	**New developments in radar technology**
Peg:	**Airline crash in India**
Longevity:	**Less than one week**

In the above real example, a mid-air crash between two planes in India sparked a rash of stories about aircraft safety. With adroit use of media contacts and/or releases it also provided an unexpected opportunity to canvass and publicise developments in radar technology. However, the media's appetite for running stories on aircraft safety was soon satisfied. It is hard to imagine interest in such a story lasting more than three or four days.

Many people who want media exposure do not understand what is news. Some news just happens: train crashes, disasters, court cases. We can be sure that these happenings will be reported on the news tonight. However, there is always space for constructed news which is actually a non-event. Here, opportunistic newsmakers step in. The successful media performer knows how to construct news. Such news usually involves the contest of ideas and points of view. This news happens when there is something at stake. It usually means there are winners and losers and people on both sides of an argument. What these newsmakers have to say will always somehow challenge the status quo. Remember that things are only news when someone gives a damn about the outcome.

To make this sort of news, you must really say something which counts. Who you are counts too. You must use your positional power in your job or in the community to give impact to what you say. That is why no one cares what I think about interest rates, but every journalist in the country stops to listen to what the Reserve Bank governor has to say on the same subject. You often need a catalyst to attract attention to your story:

- Commission research or conduct it yourself.
- Commission or conduct an opinion poll on your subject.
- Survey people affected by your issue.
- Write a book or report on the issue.
- Offer to write a feature article for a newspaper.

- Develop case studies of people affected by your issue.
- Enlist famous people to your cause.
- Cultivate some sympathetic or interested journalists.
- Become a source of valuable information.
- Stage an event with real novelty value.

The Media Release

Media releases are an important means of letting the media know that you have something to say. They are also an important means for you to organise your thoughts on paper.

The problem with media releases is that news organisations get flooded by hundreds of them each day. Making a media release cut through the noise of all the other press statements competing for attention is no easy task.

Cultivating a Relationship with a Journalist

If you have a need to communicate regularly through the media, you should get to know the journalists who cover your round. There are great advantages in building a relationship of trust with a few key journalists. A journalist who needs you as a source will think twice before sledging you in a story. If the journalist breaks your trust in them, they will pay a price by losing you as a source. A journalist with whom you have a good relationship is much less likely to portray you adversely.

With a Little Time for Preparation

When a journalist contacts you, first, you must decide whether you want to be interviewed at all—and, if so, prepare some answers. There are some simple structures for answering questions to communicate your own agenda. Once you're familiar with

them, they are perfect to use when you've had little or no warning
of an interview.

To Talk or Not to Talk

The first question to ask yourself before talking to a journalist is
whether it is in your interest to do so. I have been amazed over
the years by the number of people who have agreed to interviews
when it does not appear to be in their best interest. Radio and
television producers and newspaper journalists are often very
skilled and persuasive in talking people into agreeing to interviews.
They are often extremely persistent.

In one remarkable example, I recall a producer approaching a
Tasmanian politician to be interviewed about the fact that he had
been found out feigning a false identity on a talkback radio
program. For the life of me I could not see any advantage to the
politician in agreeing to the request. Nevertheless, he agreed. Some
time after the interview was recorded, but before it was broadcast,
the politician rang back. He pleaded that we not use part of the
interview in which he had freely admitted that it wasn't the first
time he had used false voices on talkback. In fact, the interviewer
had not even noticed the comment. Now we really had a story!
The politician should have politely declined to be interviewed in
the first place. He compounded the error by his return call. The
story may have died a natural death if he had not cooperated.

Of course, one consequence of adopting a 'repel' strategy and
refusing to be interviewed is that you may have to put up with
being named on the program: 'We contacted so and so from XYZ
corporation but he/she was unavailable'. Or, more seriously, 'but
he/she refused to comment'. Or, most seriously: 'We have made
several attempts to interview so and so but they have consistently
refused to speak to us'. Whatever your circumstances, refusing to

comment can make you appear like the guilty party. You are damned if you do, damned if you don't. Polite refusal, however, is often the right thing.

Communicating Your Agenda

The most important thing to do when speaking to a journalist is to communicate your agenda. Your agenda is your message. It should consist of only one point if it is a sound bite for news. It should never be more than three points in a longer interview. So your agenda is the list of one, two or three things you must communicate. Write them down and number them. Take the piece of paper with you if you are leaving the office to meet a journalist or have it by the telephone if you are talking to a newspaper reporter or on radio from your desk. No matter how urgent the need to speak, do not begin without taking a few minutes to nut out your agenda.

Agenda

1 . . . .
2 . . . .
3 . . . .

Do not wait to be asked about the points that you want to make. You will never be asked in direct terms. You have to be assertive about getting your agenda across or the conversation may be entirely one-sided. Most journalists have a list of simple questions to ask. The journalist may never find out what you want to talk about unless you are forceful in getting out your message. This means that you have to answer the questions you would like to be asked as well as the questions that you are asked. Without these assertive skills, you will sound only as good or bad as your

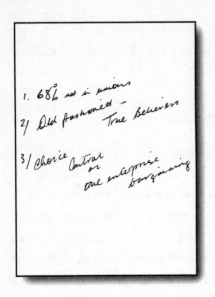

1 68% not in unions

2 Old fashioned — True believers

3 Choice: Central
   Or True enterprise bargaining

Figure 7.1 The Prime Minister writes out his agenda. So should you.

ability to respond to someone else's questions. The fact that you have your own agenda to communicate also shows that you are proactive rather than just reactive in the situation.

Q = A + 1

When Ronald Reagan was seeking a second term as president of the United States, he performed badly in the first televised debate with his opponent, Fritz Mondale. Reagan appeared tentative and uncertain of his points. He took some advice from Roger Ailes, who writes about the experience in his book, *You are the Message*. Ailes recommended that Reagan use the following simple formula to answer questions:

$$Q = A + 1$$

Your response to a question (Q) should have three elements. First, do your best to answer (A) the question which is asked.

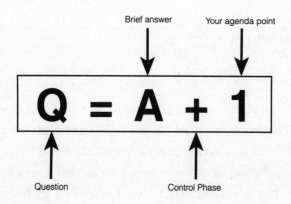

Brief answer   Your agenda point

$$Q = A + 1$$

Question   Control Phase

Figure 7.2 $Q = A + 1$

Second, you will need to use a 'control phrase' (+) to segue to your agenda point. Third, add your message (1).

Talk about your own agenda as you answer the first question. Inexperienced interviewees are shocked by how quickly the time passes when the tape or cameras are rolling. If you hesitate your moment will be lost!

Control Phrases (+)

How do you shift from answering the question to inserting your agenda? Control phrases are transition statements between the first part of your answer and your own agenda point. You should develop some control phrases of your own. Here are some samples of control phrases favoured by politicians:

The facts of the matter are . . .

. . . but an even more important question is . . .

What I want to say is this . . .

The real issue is . . .

The most important point is . . .

. . . but that is not the most critical thing . . .

> The reality is . . .
> The key to all this is . . .
> Look . . .

Don't follow the example of politicians too literally by completely ignoring the questions being asked and only talking on your own agenda points. Politicians are expert at deflection, but the well-honed filters of the media savvy audience mean they know exactly what game is being played. There are few points to be gained from ignoring every curly question or pretending it wasn't asked. Or, as one former Queensland premier used to say by way of standard reply, 'don't you worry about that'. Try to answer the question before proceeding to your agenda.

The Three Parts of an Answer

A recent participant at one of my seminars told me that: 'Even though I've already done over 100 TV interviews, 200 radio interviews and have had several hundred articles published, this workshop has been a very worthwhile experience.' What proved so worthwhile to even such an experienced media hand was learning the following simple formula for structuring an answer.

Every good answer has three parts:

- point;
- reason;
- example.

Let me illustrate with the following example:

Question: **What impact will staging the 2000 Olympics have on Australia?**

Answer:

Point:	This will be the most important international event ever held in Australia.
Reason:	That is because there are far more countries competing and far more athletes than ever before.
Example:	For example, the world television audience for the Olympics is now several billion.

In reality, what you say last—your choice of example—is likely to influence the framing of the next question. Knowing this, some interviewees will leave an important point hanging in the air. For instance, they may end their previous answer with the words: 'There are plenty of examples of that.' This begs the question: 'What examples?' It makes sense to choose your example carefully, because it will probably stimulate follow-up questions.

Of course, you don't have time to think consciously of any formula for answering questions during the helter-skelter of an interview. The time for burning this structure into your mind is before you begin. *Now* is a good time! During rehearsals for the interview which you conduct with your colleagues, stick by this structure. By the time you get to the real thing, you'll know it subconsciously.

Once you have briefly worked through the three parts of the structure, shut up. Avoid the temptation to go on too long. It is the interviewer's job to fill the silence. They will soon come up with the next question.

The Quotable Quote and the Irresistible Sound Bite

What are you going to say in your next interview which will really ram your message home? What is your quotable quote?

What will be memorable about what you say? What will make your message condensed and forceful?

The Clever One-liner

To control the outcome so that the journalist is attracted to what you really want reported, you must construct your sound bite to be the most expressive thing you say. Like a bait, it will hook the attention of the audience. Metaphors create focus, so they make great sound bites. A well-chosen image will sum up your case in a few succinct words. Tony Blair did it with the catchphrase 'twenty-two Tory tax rises'. Remember, too, the famous phrase used by lawyer Johnny Cochran in concluding the defence for O.J. Simpson: 'If it doesn't fit, you must acquit.' He was referring to the glove which O.J. had allegedly worn during the murders. At his trial, Simpson had tried on the glove, but it was too small. The fit of the glove became a metaphor for the fit of the other evidence.

The BBC called Cochran's image a master stroke. *Time* reported that the slogan and the idea behind it proved pivotal. The words had been thought up by defence lawyer Gerald Uelman, who said: 'What I was really proposing was that it would provide a good theme for the whole argument, because so much of the other circumstantial evidence didn't fit the prosecution's scenario.' A good sound bite will always sum up your case.

People in the know often set up their sound bites. Tell the audience it's coming as JFK did: 'And so my fellow Americans . . .' It gets the journalist and audience to listen more carefully to what's following. Other simple phrases which can set up your quotable quote are: 'Look . . .', 'It all boils down to . . .', 'To sum it all up . . .', 'This is the real point . . .', 'The heart of this issue is . . .'.

Some great quotable quotes:

A house divided against itself cannot stand. I believe this government cannot endure permanently half slave and half free
Abraham Lincoln, June 1858

What is good for the country is good for General Motors,
and what's good for General Motors is good for the country.
Charles Erwin Wilson, to US Senate Committee, 1952

The buck stops here.
President Harry Truman summing up his philosophy of office

Well may he say God save the Queen because no one will
save the Governor General.
Gough Whitlam, 11 November 1975

We'll just end up being a third rate economy . . . a banana
republic.
Paul Keating, May 1986

I want to be the Queen of Hearts.
Diana, Princess of Wales, in BBC interview, 1995

Few, if any, of the great quotes are spontaneous. Churchill understood that the best spontaneous quotes are always well rehearsed.
Occasionally you may have the good luck to create a memorable
line on the run. However, most good quotes are the result of
focused creative thinking. Ideas to help you prepare a memorable
line are contained in Chapter 3. When you have devised your
sound bite, rehearse it out loud before you speak to the journalist.

The Timed Sound Bite

The art of the sound bite or quotable quote is not only being colourful but also succinct. The quotable quote that the newspaper journalist wants is really only one or two sentences which expressively sum up the story. The fifteen seconds which the radio news journalist wants could be the same few sentences you give to the newspaper journalist. The six seconds which the television news journalist wants is one sentence or even as little as a phrase to sum up the story.

The way to control the sound bite or quotable quote is to make it riveting. It has to be the most expressively interesting thing you say. You need to prepare carefully to ensure that your message stands out from the rest of what you say to the journalist. You must then say it in the interview, come what may!

Most journalists looking only for a sound bite will end the interview once they have what they want. Typically, the journalist will ask you a few questions and at the same time be listening carefully to see how your answers can be tailored to their story.

Australia's deputy prime minister, Tim Fischer, is a master of the sound bite. He says sound bites can be a positive in giving people a clear-cut message. He shared his talent for tailoring his message to the time available in a discussion with Agnes Cusack on Radio National's *Media Report*. He used as an example how he would respond to a question about whether Medicare should support the IVF program being used by lesbian couples. He began with a fifteen-second sound bite which would be suitable for radio:

Yes, of course we should tolerate homosexual and lesbian gay couples and they should be allowed to go about their lives. But that does not mean that they have a right, at taxpayers' expense, to obtain designer children and do so under the IVF program.

Moments later, Tim Fischer reduced this message down to the five-second version suitable for television:

Of course, we should tolerate gays but that does not mean we have to fund their child-bearing whims.

Discipline Your Message

Experienced communicators learn the art of self-discipline. If you have one message that you want to communicate, then do not be distracted into answering a question that does not relate to your message. This is the essence of being in control.

Michael Deaver, Ronald Reagan's one-time deputy chief of staff, advises his high-profile public relations clients that no matter what the product is, the recipe for communication success is the same: discipline, focus, repetition.

Look at the following exercise in message focus and discipline being practised by Bob Carr, the New South Wales premier. It was broadcast as part of a Radio National *Background Briefing* on the premier. This is Bob Carr's telephone conversation with an ABC radio news journalist. His repetition of the one point gives the journalist no option about which message to broadcast in the news sound bite.

Bob Carr:	**Loud and clear? OK. You can say that the premier, Bob Carr, said this morning that the government would proceed with its bed tax proposal as part of the budget legislation in**

the state upper house. I'll give you a grab to go with that . . .

Well, we've asked the . . . Start that again . . . We're asking the taxpayers to put $620 million into Olympic construction this year, and at the same time, we as a government are putting computers into schools, expanding the hospitals' budget and putting extra police on the beat. Frankly, the big city hotels ought to be making a modest contribution to a budget which has funded the Olympics but maintains essential social infrastructure.

Journalist: So, you'll be standing firm on this?

Bob Carr: Well, we're asking the taxpayers generally to put over $600 million into Olympic construction, and at the same time, we're maintaining the social expenditure of New South Wales with increases in the budget for hospitals, for schools and for police. Frankly, the big city hotels ought to make the modest contribution. They, after all, are the industry sector that will do most handsomely out of the Games.

Journalist: So, there won't be any negotiation?

Bob Carr: No. See you later. Bye.

Journalist: [after disconnection, chuckling] Can't believe it.

There you have it. Discipline, focus, repetition.

No comment

If you don't have a choice in the matter and the microphone is already on, when should you say 'no comment'? There is no simple answer to this question, as it will depend on the circumstances. A situation of personal distress is one good example of when you should be extremely cautious. Insist on your right to privacy unless it is an issue of corporate responsibility. If there is no option but to make some statement about an accident at work or whatever, you have every right to name when and in what form the statement will be made.

Answering possibly defamatory allegations against you requires great caution. If the story is wrong you must say so to a journalist but agreeing to answer allegations can sometimes simply amplify them.

Sound Bite Rules

In delivering a sound bite, you need to bear a few rules in mind.

- Write down your sound bite on paper. Memorise it.
- Tailor your message to the length needed. Newspapers want a few sentences for a quote, radio about fifteen seconds for news, television about six seconds for news.
- On radio and television, try to encapsulate the question in the answer. It makes it vastly easier for editing by saving the journalist the need to set up the question in their script. For example:

  Question: What have you decided?

  Answer: We've decided that . . .
- End your sound bite on a downward inflection. Keep your sentences disciplined. Sentences need a clear starting and ending point.
- Make your body language work during the sound bite. Where appropriate, be passionate.

Metaphors and Anecdotes Make Sound Bites

In Chapter 3, I referred to Ray Martin's reply to the question about the best people he had ever interviewed. He mentioned Peter Ustinov, David Suzuki and a few others. Martin summed up by saying: 'They are anecdote machines.'

To make people remember what you say, you need to become an anecdote machine too. Drive what you say by stories and examples. Use images and metaphors. Refer to Chapter 3 for ideas about how to construct effective sound bites.

The Double/Triple Whammy Sound Bite

A double whammy is simply repeating the same form of words; a triple whammy repeats them again.

Example of repetition:
Veni, vidi, vici.

Julius Caesar, at Zela, 47BC

I cannot forecast to you the action of Russia. It is a riddle, wrapped in a mystery, inside an enigma.

Winston Churchill, 1 October 1939

Compelling Comparisons as Sound Bites

Finding just the right evidence and presenting it effectively can be very persuasive. The campaign to stop tobacco sponsorship of sport made a huge leap forward when Ros Kelly, the then federal sports minister, was presented with a graph showing that more kids in New South Wales smoked Winfield while more kids in Victoria smoked Peter Jackson. The two brands were the major football sponsors in each state. Kelly says her mind was made up by this simple evidence.

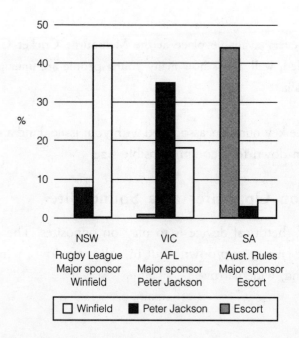

Figure 7.2 12–14 Year Olds: What they smoked in 1984
Source: Sydney Morning Herald, 2 April 1992

Never underestimate the power of simple facts and compelling comparisons. They become hard stories to beat.

Getting Numbers Down to Size as a Sound Bite

Few people can grapple with the real meaning of big numbers.

I recall a Melbourne *Age* story on the current account deficit which reported that, in the month just ended, for every dollar Australia spent abroad, we earned only 94 cents. It was a powerful means of making a multi-billion dollar figure seem comprehensible at the simplest level.

Example:

Imagine every available place at the Melbourne Cricket Ground being filled, well, that's how many young people are unemployed in Australia.

Think of the key numbers associated with your issue. Find a means to get them down to a comprehensible size.

Playing on Opposites as a Sound Bite

A powerful rhetorical device is to play on opposites. The possibilities are many: up/down, out/in, above/below, win/lose, ahead/behind, wide/narrow.

Example:

Unemployment is up, hope is down.
As the budget blows out, belts have to come in.

Spend a few moments creating 'opposites' to add rhetorical spice to a key message in your news grab.

Rhyming Language as a Sound Bite

Search for language which rhymes like a chime. A useful asset is a rhyming dictionary, organised around the rhymes of final syllables.

Example:

All the way with LBJ.

Spend a few moments creating rhyme in a key sentence of your message.

Ambushes and the Difficult Questions

The Doorstop Interview or Ambush

Sound bites are often delivered at doorstop interviews. The rapid movement of these encounters lends itself to the drama of news reporting on television and radio. The experienced media handler exercises considerable control at the doorstop interview by walking away when they have finished what they want to say. In politics, many of these doorstops are planned by ministers whose staff notify journalists that they will be available for a doorstop. The politicians come ready with their sound bite. Less often, the doorstop can take the form of an ambush where the person being confronted has no idea of what's coming.

Practise, practise, practise

Even a self-confident performer like Margaret Thatcher would set aside several hours to rehearse her answers to likely questions in parliament. Her apparent spontaneity was nothing of the sort. Her onstage performances reflected her preparation offstage.

The best way to handle tough questions is to anticipate them. Work with a colleague before the interview and brainstorm what would be the most difficult questions. Write them down. Write out possible answers using the point, reason, example structure discussed earlier. Then rehearse your answers out loud.

You Don't Need to Answer the Question

Many interviewees act as though they are in a court of law under cross-examination when speaking in a television or radio interview. You are not. You do not have to answer the questions that are put to you. There may be any number of reasons why it is inappropriate to answer the questions. These may include issues of confidentiality, privacy, defamation, or sub judice. It may be just plain bad politics to answer a direct question on a sensitive subject. Whatever the reason, you firmly and politely say that you will not answer the question.

You might employ a two-stage strategy to a question you don't want to answer. In stage one, simply ignore or deflect the question. In stage two, if the interviewer is being persistent about it, state that you will not answer the question. You may give a reason if it feels appropriate. If the journalist is like a terrier and won't leave the bone alone, use the broken record technique: say again and again you will not answer the question. Stick by your resolve.

Avoid Loaded Words

Words are bullets in the media. Sometimes words will be used in a question that you should never repeat in your response even if only to rebut them. Examples of loaded words are disaster, mismanagement, disorganised, disillusioned, corrupt, unhappy and bankrupt. Never get set up by a question such as, 'Isn't this mismanagement?' by saying in reply, 'It is not mismanagement'. The editing process will simply use your reply and expose you to damage from your own words. If you doubt this, try not thinking of a black cat. The mere suggestion of a black cat puts the image in your mind, even if I am telling you not to think of a black cat. Likewise, if the audience hears the word 'mismanagement', the smell of 'mismanagement' lingers. When loaded words are thrown at you, ignore them.

Rebut Wrong Information

Although you should side-step loaded words, you must confront wrong information or assumptions contained in a question. If you do not challenge error, it becomes a truth. Go straight to the error with words such as: 'What you are saying is wrong.' In radio and television interviews, challenge the errors at the first opportunity you get.

'Off the Record'

You need to be wary when journalists use terms like 'off the record'. What do you think it means? The problem is it means different things to different journalists. To some it means that what you say to them will be treated purely as background and you will not be quoted. To others it means that you can be quoted but not by name. However, what you say in these situations may give away your identity anyhow. It is safest to assume when you are talking to a journalist that whatever you say may end up in print. You may be quoted from the moment you answer the telephone until the moment you hang up.

What Do You Do if Things Go Badly Wrong

I referred at the beginning of the chapter to a man who had the appalling experience of his mind going blank while being interviewed for a television current affairs program. In the midst of a long interview being conducted out of doors on a hot day, he lost his train of thought. The interviewer tried to be helpful. He prompted him a few times. Still silence. At last the man was ready to talk again. He said: 'We can roll again now.' What he didn't know was that the camera hadn't stopped rolling. The next night, the whole unedited sequence was shown.

Leaving aside the ethical question about whether the network should have shown this sequence, what might the man have done to prevent it?

The first step is not to take the good faith of the interviewer or television program for granted. The man did not ask that the offending section not be shown. No one from his office did anything for 24 hours. At this late stage, a phone call was made to the program asking whether this lapse would be deleted. By then a decision had presumably been made to show it.

Everyone has lapses. If you lose your train of thought or something else goes seriously wrong, ask on the spot to be given another chance to get it right. The professional interviewees get away with it, why can't you? Your chances of being treated fairly in this situation will increase immensely if you are going to be of some future use to the journalist and if you remain cool. If the journalist on the spot is unhelpful, call their boss. Should you go further by taking out an injunction to stop the media from showing something after you have agreed to an interview? You are probably wasting your time and money, but if you really must, ask your lawyer.

Persuasive Body Language on Television

Many people who appear in the media are so focused on their content that they are unaware of the messages being sent by their body language and tone of voice. Body language and voice reveal how you feel about what you are saying. Your audience will place more trust in *how* you say something than *what* you say.

Appearing in the media is a performance. For many people, it is also an anxious experience which makes them retreat into defensive and negative body language. You need a positive and persuasive repertoire of gestures to show confidence in yourself and your message. You need to 'free' yourself in order to be yourself!

On television, you are inviting yourself into someone's lounge-room. Your body language and voice need to reflect the intimate surroundings in which you are talking to your one-on-one audience.

You may encounter hostile questions. It is vital that you do not allow your feelings towards the interviewer to become your message to the audience.

As you begin a media appearance, remember to 'lighten up'. Remember too that, in the media, everything needs to be a bit bigger than in everyday life.

Eyes

- Keep eye contact with the interviewer only.
- Open your eyes wide. Eyebrow movement can help.
- Be so alive that your eyes sparkle.
- Do not look at the camera. Do not create a shifty eye look by glancing back and forth between the interviewer and the camera.
- Avoid wearing glasses that reflect television lights.

Head and Face

- Smile. This gesture will win more friends and warm up your interview more than anything you say.
- Allow yourself to laugh.
- Feel free to sometimes nod to acknowledge the question, even if you disagree with the proposition.
- Avoid frowning even though the matter you are discussing is serious.
- Don't hold your head rigidly.

Hands and Arms

- Use your hands to get your meaning out. Hand movement will help animate your voice, face and body.
- Keep your hand movements below the conventional head and shoulders camera shot. Do not obscure your face with your hands.

Standing

- Try a quick relaxation exercise as the crew prepares its equipment.
- Avoid folding your arms and crossing your hands behind your back or in front of your crotch.

Sitting

- Sit slightly forward. It shows engagement.
- Sit on the tail of your jacket to stop it riding up over your shoulders.
- Avoid swivelling in the chair.
- Do not fold your arms or cross your hands in your lap.

Practise Being Interviewed

- Assess your performances. Get a trusted colleague to give you specific feedback about your body language.
- You will benefit from prior practice as you seek to improve the confidence of your on-stage body language. The bathroom mirror and videotaping yourself are good ways to start.

Being open in your own body language will not always be to your advantage. There will be times when it is better to obscure how you really feel (if you can).

Dress and Appearance

Dress and grooming are an important part of the non-verbal message that you send on television. Your objective should be to make the audience feel comfortable with you.

What is 'comfortable' for an audience? In general, the answer is what an audience expects. If you are a minister in the government, then the audience expects you to wear a suit Monday to Friday and more casual clothes on Saturday and Sunday. If you are in tropical climates, that's different. You can dress for a tropical climate in a businesslike way. If you are in rural Australia, you can dress more casually than if you are in urban Australia.

Sometimes an important message can be sent by not dressing in the way an audience expects. Breaking stereotypes can be powerful. During the Franklin River conservation campaign in Tasmania, the green campaigners went to considerable lengths to urge protesters to dress conservatively. The object was to allow audiences to see their mirror image, people who appeared just like themselves on the television screen. The message was to appear absolutely mainstream and non-threatening. As a tactic, it worked. On the other hand, some conservation campaigns have been handicapped by featuring television coverage of alternative lifestylers who can all too easily be dismissed by a middle class audience as 'not one of us'.

A Few Basic Rules

- On television, white shirts can fuzz and sharp pinstripes can flare. Avoid wearing them where possible. Pastel colours are good for shirts.
- Dark, solid colours look best in suits.
- Avoid tartans and large checks.
- Shave off the beard. With rare exceptions, they hide the face and get in the way of open communication.
- Audiences tend not to trust men in bowties.
- Earrings and jewellery need to be conservative so that they do not distract attention.
- Higher necklines usually flatter women on television.
- If you normally wear glasses, think about whether you need

them for the interview, whether you look better with them on or off. If you appear regularly and need to wear glasses, make sure the frames are large enough not to hide your eyes. Adjustments can be made to frames to avoid studio lighting glare.

- Avoid glasses which tint in the light.

Some people who never know when a television interview may occur next keep a change of clothes in their office wardrobe. Wear clothes you feel good in. Clothes selection is important but remember that your expression is the most important thing that you wear.

Summary: Dealing with the Media to Communicate Your Message

Before the Interview

- Research the purpose and likely duration of the interview; think about your audience.
- Decide whether you should agree to the interview. Will it serve your interests?
- Develop one message for a news interview and up to three agenda points or messages for a longer interview. Write them down.
- Write one key supporting argument for each point or message.
- Write down the examples you want to use.
- Develop your quotable quote.
- Anticipate the most difficult questions. How would you answer them? Rehearse with colleagues.
- Practise relaxation and voice warm-up exercises.

During the Interview

- Be positive—particularly when you are on the defensive.
- Remember Q = A + 1. Answer the question and use it as a springboard to raise your agenda points. Don't just be reactive to questions.
- Use the point, reason, example structure.
- Come alive. Animate your face and voice. Be passionate. Smile and lighten up. Enjoy it!
- Keep your answers short.
- Communicate person to person—your audience is no bigger than a few people in one place.
- Be an anecdote machine: use parables, anecdotes, metaphors and draw on personal experiences.

After the Interview

- Analyse whether you communicated your key messages.
- Assess your performance and draw lessons for future reference.
- Observe radio and television programs—learn to model the behaviour of effective communicators.

FURTHER READING

Ailes, Roger, *You are the Message*, New York: Doubleday, 1988.

Aristotle, *The Art of Rhetoric*, London: Penguin, 1991.

Fisher, Roger and Ury, William, *Getting to Yes*, Sydney: Century Hutchinson Australia, 1981.

Kennedy, George A., *A New History of Classical Rhetoric*, Princeton: Princeton University Press, 1994.

Minto, Barbara, *The Pyramid Principle*, London: Minto International, 1987.

Satir, Virginia, *People Making*, Palo Alto: Science and Behaviour Books, 1972.

Thompson, Peter, *The Secrets of the Great Communicators*, Sydney: ABC Books, 1992.

Zelazny, Gene, *Say it with Charts*, Homewood, Ill.: Business One Irwin, 1991.

INDEX

Index compiled by Russell Brooks

answer format for presentations 36–7
arguments
  constructing 34–5
  deductive 30
  inductive 30–2
arrangement 5–6, 16, 99–101
artistic persuasion 7–10
auditor personality type 72–5, 123, 146
auditory senses 42, 43

Beazley, Kim 76
Bell, John 11–13, 57–8
Bjelke-Petersen, Joh 67
Black, Conrad 70
Blair, Tony 55, 194
body language
  persuasive 119, 120–2, 150–3
  and television 206–8
brain, switching on the whole 39–41
Branson, Richard 66
Brown, Senator Bob 76
business presentation 7, 87–130
  arrangement and *logos* 99–101
  body language 120–5
  breathing and voice exercises 126–7
  charts and speaker aids 103–18
  delivery and *pathos* 118–20

invention 94–9
  non-verbal messages and personality 122–3
  performance anxiety 125–8
  persuasive 93–130
  picture your audience 97–9
  and rehearsing 123–5
  style and *pathos* 101–2
  summary 128–30
  using notes 127–8
Button, John 76
Buttrose, Ita 70

Carlopio, James 13
Carr, Bob 74
Carville, James 33–4
character 7, 8
charts 106–12
Churchill, Winston 14, 18, 47, 53
Clancy, John 52
Clinton, Hillary 70
Cohen, Herb 149
communicating your agenda 189–93
communication 40, 42
  capacity for playing opposites 78–83
  cross-cultural 32–3
  non-verbal 118–20, 122–3
  persuasive 6–7

style profiles 64–78, 83
communicator personality type
  65–8, 122, 145
confirmatio 17
conflict 133
Confucius 38, 42
Costello, Peter 70
Court, Richard 74

Dalai Lama 77
Deane, Sir William 73
delivery 6–7, 118–20
Doogue, Geraldine 77
Downer, Alexander 76
Dunlap, Al 69–70

Einstein, Albert 101
Elliott, John 70
ethos 7, 8, 11, 15, 95–7, 136
exordium 17

Fahey, John 76
Farrahkan, Lewis 67
Fischer, Tim 76
Fisher, Roger 138
five-point plan of persuasion 18–28
four-part story of letters of proposal
  28, 29–30
Fraser, Bernie 73

Galton, Sir Francis 62
Gandhi, Mahatma 77
Gates, Bill 66
George, Jennie 76
Gorton, John 76
Graham, Billy 20
Greiner, Nick 74

Hagberg, Richard 73
Harvey, Geoff 66
Hawke, Bob 67, 76
Hayden, Bill 76

Hill, David 70
Hitler, Adolf 18
Holmes à Court, Janet 76
Howard, John 74
Hughes, Tom 33
humour 54–6

invention 5, 94–9

Johnson, Samuel 140
Jones, Caroline 77
Jones, Clare 87, 88–93, 101, 123
Joss, Bob 73
Jung, Carl Gustav 62–3, 64–5

Keating, Paul 50–1, 70, 184
Kelty, Bill 76
Kennett, Jeff 67
Kernot, Cheryl 76
key points 33–4
Keynes, John Maynard 53
kinesthetic senses 42–3, 44
King, Martin Luther 18, 67
Kipling, Rudyard 39
Kramer, Dame Leonie 70

language
  body 119, 120–5, 150–3,
    206–8
  persuasive 38–9
Lee Kuan Yew 70
letters of proposal 28–30
Levi-Strauss, Claude 47
Lock, Simon 67
Locke, John 38
logos 7, 9, 11, 15, 71, 74, 99–101,
    103–18, 136, 142
Lumby, Catherine 47–8

McKinsey and Co 16, 25, 28, 29
Mandela, Nelson 77
Mason, Sir Anthony 73

media 166–211
  ambushes and difficult questions
    203–6
  communicate your message 210–11
  communicating your agenda 189–93
  discipline your message 197–8
  dress and appearance 208–10
  journalists 174–84
  and metaphors 200
  news 184–8
  newspaper journalists 182–4
  no comment 198–9
  picture your audience 173–4
  quotable quote 193–203
  radio journalists 180–2
  tailoring your message 172–3
  talk or not to talk 188–9
  television journalists 178–80
  television and body language
    206–8
  timed sound bite 196–7, 199–202
  your audience 168–71
Mehrabian, Albert 119
memory 6
metaphor 23, 46–8
  Biblical 48–9
  and business presentation 101–2
  in business and economics 51–2
  and images 54–9
  and media 200
  and negotiation 161
  in politics 50–1
  Shakespeare 49–50
  sources of 52–4
Mitsui, Cathy 51
Murdoch, Rupert 70
Murray, David 73
Myers-Briggs Type Indicator 63

narratio 17
negotiation 131–65
  aggressive behaviour 156–7

agreement 162, 165
ambit claims 157–8
bad cop/good cop 155–6
building rapport 148–53
closing a deal 163–4
conflict and competition 133
deadlines 159–60
deadlock 162–3
defined 135–6
doggedly optimistic 160
equal time 157
five principles 136–41
framework 146–8
higher authority 155
integrative versus distributive
  strategies 134
last-minute claims 154–5
making concessions 158–9
metaphor to reframe 161
model 131–3
positive tactics 160
preparing for 142–4
and relationships 134–5
scarcity 158
stages 146–8, 153–63
styles 145–6
tactics at the table 153–63
turning a deaf ear 161–2
value of service declines 158
neurolinguistic programming (NLP)
  42–3
Nixon, Richard 184
non-verbal
  communication 118–20, 122–3
  messages and personality 122–3
notes and business presentations
  127–8
Nugent, Helen 25–6

passion 7, 9–10
pathos 7, 9–10, 11, 15, 67, 101–2,
  118–20, 136

performance anxiety 125–8
peroratio 17–18
persuasion 7–10, 33
  and different personalities 60–86
  five-point plan 18–28
  in Greece and Rome 16–18
persuasive
  being wholly 58–9
  body language 119, 120–2
  business presentation 93–125,
    128–30
  conceptual framework 15–16
  language 101–2
personalities
  auditors 72–5, 123, 146
  capacity for playing opposites
    78–83
  communication style profiles
    64–78, 83
  communicators 65–8, 122, 145
  different 60–86
  and non-verbal messages 122–3
  self assessment 83–5
  shakers 68–72, 122–3, 145–6
  sharers 75–8, 123, 146
  styles 63–4
  types 65–78, 145
Peters, Tom 60–2, 66, 70
Plato 2, 3
presentations 36–7
probatio 17

questions
  answering 35–6
  for presentations 36–7
  see also media

Reagan, Ronald 67, 76, 78
reasoning 7, 9
rehearsing 123–5

rhetoric 16–18
  five principles 5–7
Roddick, Anita 66

Satir, Virginia 122
senses, the 42–4
shaker personality type 68–72,
  122–3, 145–6
Shakespeare, William 49–50
sharer personality types 75–8, 123,
  146
Simon, Paul 76
Singleton, John 67
Smith, Adam 47
Smith, Dick 66
Socrates 2, 3–4
speaker aids 103–18
Sperry, Roger 40
storytelling 56–8
Strong, James 76
style 6, 101–2
Sun Tsu 52

technology and business
  presentations 112–18
Teresa, Mother 77
Thatcher, Margaret 70

Ury, William 138, 162

visual senses 42, 43
voice exercises 126–7

Wedgwood, Josiah 53
Whitlam, Gough 67
Willis, Ralph 51
word pictures, creating 45–6
Wran, Neville 70

Zelazny, Gene 104